W9-BKF-687

THE TRUE STORY OF

MARY, WIFE OF LINCOLN

(COVER)

The portrait of Mary Todd Lincoln was painted by Francis B. Carpenter, the same artist who painted Abraham Lincoln reading the Emancipation Proclamation to his cabinet. The Mary Lincoln portrait was started in early 1865 and was commissioned by Mrs. Lincoln herself. It was to be a surprise for her husband. When President Lincoln was assassinated, the portrait was incomplete. Mr. Carpenter presented the finished painting to Mrs. Lincoln later that year.

This artistic piece is now owned by the Illinois State Historical Society and is on permanent loan to the Governor's Mansion in Springfield.

MARY TODD LINCOLN

The above photograph of an oil painting done by the author, Katherine Helm. The original oil of Mary Todd Lincoln now hangs in the Lincoln Bedroom of the White House.

THE TRUE STORY OF
MARY, WIFE OF LINCOLN

*Containing the Recollections of Mary Lincoln's
Sister Emilie (Mrs. Ben Hardin Helm), Extracts
from Her War-Time Diary, Numerous Letters
and Other Documents now First Published*

By Her Niece, KATHERINE HELM

Preface by Jean H. Baker

*"Lady of Lincoln,
They wreathed her head
With thorns when living,
With nettles though dead."*

MARION MILLS MILLER

WITH MANY ILLUSTRATIONS

NEW YORK AND LONDON
HARPER & BROTHERS PUBLISHERS
MCMXXVIII

▼

MARY, WIFE OF LINCOLN
COPYRIGHT, 1928, BY KATHERINE HELM
PRINTED IN THE U. S. A.
FIRST EDITION
SECOND EDITION
THIRD EDITION PRINTED BY
WF SHARP AND COMPANY PRINTERS,
RUTLAND, VERMONT
FOR FRIENDS OF HILDENE, INC.
MANCHESTER, VERMONT
2005

TO

MRS. ROBERT TODD LINCOLN

WHO LOVED

MARY TODD LINCOLN

THIS BOOK IS

AFFECTIONATELY DEDICATED

CONTENTS

ILLUSTRATIONS

MARY

WIFE OF LINCOLN

Preface To Second Edition

It is fitting that modern readers have an opportunity to appreciate Katherine Helm's classic biography of Mary Todd Lincoln. Published in 1928 amid favorable reviews that acknowledged it as well-written, "interesting and infinitely moving," *Mary, Wife of Lincoln* has been out of print for over half a century. On many counts it merits a second printing.

As Mary Lincoln's niece, Katherine Helm was privy to the remembrance of her mother Emilie Todd Helm who was Mary's favorite half-sister, as well as to her own associations with her famous aunt. But Helm also had access to family diaries, letters and documents, and was, in fact, the only author with whom the Lincoln family cooperated. Throughout her life Helm who was born in 1857 and died in 1937 maintained a close relationship with Mary Lincoln's only surviving son Robert and his wife Mary Harlan Lincoln. A talented writer and painter who completed six oil portraits of Mary Todd Lincoln, Katherine Helm was a logical choice to write a biography of her celebrated aunt. The result is an important corrective to some of the vicious portrayals of Mary Lincoln's character and behavior that still persist in contemporary Lincoln studies.

Like Mary Lincoln's life, *Mary, Wife of Lincoln* falls into three sections—Mary as a Todd in Lexington, Kentucky and Springfield, Illinois, Mary as the wife of Lincoln in Illinois and in Washington where the author came as a six-year old during the Civil War when her recently widowed mother needed a pass to move through Union lines, and finally a short section of mostly letters covering the final years of Mary Lincoln's life after her husband's assassination in 1865 until her death in 1882. Helm's contribution rests in the first two sections of the book where her intimate association with relatives as well as her first-hand knowledge of Kentucky as a Todd and a Helm provided her with a natural understanding of her subject's life. The Mary Lincoln that emerges in *Mary, Wife of Lincoln* is a vivacious, intelligent and engaging woman—"Light-hearted but not Light-headed."

There are points that some historians may dispute such as Helm's depiction of Lincoln's visit to Columbia, Missouri in the summer of 1840 to court Mary and the author's omission of the Lincoln's move to the cottage on South Fourth Street in Springfield. Still the picture of a beleaguered woman whose head, in the epigram Helm chooses, was wreathed by public opinion "in thorns and nettles" is valid. Whatever outsiders saw in Mary Todd Lincoln, the family, including the husband who loved her, enjoyed a gay, warm-hearted, and sensitive human being.

Jean H. Baker
Professor of History
Goucher College, 1999

The True Story of

MARY, WIFE OF LINCOLN

꧁꧂

CHAPTER I

A VIVID LITTLE PERSON

A SMALL white pony galloped down the shady street, on his back a slender thirteen-year-old girl. Through the town and out along the dusty highway leading to "Ashland," they raced, the child's short, clustering light brown curls blown back by the swift movement of the pony shining gold and bronze in the brilliant sunlight. The strings of her ruffled white sunbonnet were tied loosely under her chin—a very determined little chin—and the sunbonnet, pushed back from her vivid rosy face, hung flapping down her back. About a mile from the town of Lexington she brought her pony to an abrupt halt before the handsome home of Mr. Henry Clay, and to the servant who appeared she requested an immediate audience with the great statesman.

"But," expostulated the old butler, "Mr. Clay is entertaining five or six fine gentlemens."

Still the child persisted; so the old servant disappeared, soon returning to say that Mr. Clay begged to be excused, for he was entertaining distinguished strangers. It was then the child threw back her head, imperiously announcing: "I can't help that. I've come all the way out to Ashland to show Mr. Clay my new pony. You go right back and tell him that *Mary Todd* would like him to step out here for a moment."

Mr. Clay, tall, suave, polished in mind and manner, came out on the graveled driveway to greet his imperious little friend, the entire company trooping after. "Look, Mr. Clay," she began, "my new pony. Father bought him from those strolling players that were stranded here last week. He can dance—look!" The proud little owner touched the pony with a whip and up he went gracefully on his hind legs. The strangers laughed as Mary exclaimed, "Mr. Clay, my father says you are the best judge of horse-flesh in Fayette County. What do you think about this pony?" "He seems as spirited as his present diminutive jockey. I am sure nothing in the state can outdistance him," answered the courteous Mr. Clay. Then lifting Mary off the pony, "You are just in time for dinner." "Yes, and just in time," said Mrs. Clay, appearing at that moment, "to take a message to your mother. I was just about to send her a letter from her uncle Mr. James Brown, but now you may take it to her after dinner."

Mary, not at all abashed at rushing into dinner without a previous invitation, resigned her beloved pony to a negro boy, and, holding tightly to Mr. Clay's hand, went into the dining room where, seated by her hero, she was blissfully happy listening with absorbed interest to the political discussion which animated the voices and faces of the diners.

During a lull she exclaimed, suddenly, "Mr. Clay, my father says you will be the next President of the United States. I wish I could go to Washington and live in the White House," she added wistfully. "I begged my father to be President but he only laughed and said he would rather see you there than to be President himself. He must like you more than he does himself. My father is a very, very peculiar man, Mr. Clay. I don't think he really wants to be President," said Mary, a note of disapproval in her voice. "Well," laughed Mr. Clay, "if I am ever President I shall expect Mary Todd to be one of my first guests. Will you come?"

Mary accepted with enthusiasm.

"If you were not already married," she said, graciously, "I would wait for you."

Mary felt this time that the burst of laughter must be at her expense.

"So I must go now," she said slipping from her chair. "Poor mother is sick in bed, Father is in Frankfort. Mammy told me I might ride the pony for a little while in front of our house. I've been gone a long time. Mammy will be wild! When I put salt in her coffee this morning she called me a limb of Satan and said I was loping down the broad road leading to destruction."

Mary dimpled into a little one-sided smile. "But Mammy is a good old soul and promised to let me hold Baby Sam for ten or fifteen minutes if I didn't squirm too much. You have seen our new baby, Mrs. Clay? Don't you think he is too soft to be very healthy? I can't help but think he needs more starch. Teeny-weeny Margaret is all right, but Sam is flimsy."

Then dropping a demure little curtsy to Mr. and Mrs. Clay, she drawled in inimitable mimicry of a well-known society belle of the day: "Thank you so much for your charming hospitality; I've had a most delightful time."

And with a mischievous glance at Mr. Clay, who had recognized the original of her caricature and was laughing heartily, Mary was gone like a flash.

Perhaps a psychoanalyst might discover in this adventure of Mary's the seed of ambition planted in her subconscious mind to grow into a wish to be mistress in the White House, at any rate she is often quoted as having said that she would marry a President of the United States.

And little Mary Todd, the future wife of Abraham Lincoln, rode home on her new pony.

CHAPTER II

TOD, in the north of England and Scotland, is "fox." It is surmised that the first man to whom the surname Todd was given was a keen sportsman who followed the hounds in the hue and cry of chasing a tod—was a tod hunter. Indeed, Toddhunter was another surname assumed by, or given to, one of these Nimrods—an amusing story told of a market gardener of Middlesex might indicate that the name had something to do with the sly wit of a fox. The gardener being haled before a magistrate for not having painted on his cart, his name, his place of residence, and the words, "taxed cart," declared he had complied with the law in every particular and invited the Court to inspect his cart upon which was painted:

"A most Odd Act on a taxed Cart"

This did not mollify the Court until it was explained to him that it could be interpreted:

"Amos Todd. Acton. A taxed Cart."

Among the Todds whose names are well known are: James Henthorn Todd, one of the best known Irish scholars of his day (born 1805); he was consulted by both statesmen and theologians. Henry John Todd edited Johnson's Dictionary to which he added several thousand words. He was also editor of Milton. Robert Bentley Todd was a physician of great renown in the early part of the nineteenth century. His statue may be seen at King's College Hospital. David Todd, with a world-wide reputation as an astronomer.

The "Mary" of Coleridge's verse was Mary Evans Todd, the mother of Elliott D'Arcy Todd of Yorkshire, the stronghold of the Todds for centuries. In the west riding of Yorkshire the town of Todmorden, dating back prior to the reign of Edward III, may have some connection with the family of that name. Among the Pilgrim Fathers from Yorkshire was Christopher Todd. He was the son of William Todd, who was the son of William Todd. He, with his wife Grace and several children, came over about 1639. He was an important personage in New Haven, of which he was one of the founders. Yale College now stands on the site of his home, and the college campus was part of Christopher's estate. Many of his descendants live in New Haven. He bore for arms three foxes' heads—showing the origin of the name.

John Todd also came from Yorkshire. He and his wife Susannah and their six children settled in Rowley, Massachusetts, 1637. He was representative to the

General Court for many years. He bore for arms a fox rampant with a dove for crest, and the motto: "By cunning. Not by Craft."

Adam Todd was born in the Highlands of Scotland. He made New York his home, and died in 1765. His wife Sarah was one of the "Women of the Revolution." Her house on Cliff Street in the city of New York was called "rebel headquarters" by the British, who said of her daughters, "They are the d—— rebels in New York." Some British soldiers in her house were drinking and asked her for a toast. "Why, we eat toast," she replied with so much simplicity that they supposed her ignorant of the meaning of the word. Mrs. Todd's grave is in St. Paul's churchyard, New York City. Her daughter Sarah married a Brevoort, one of the family whose name is perpetuated in many ways in the metropolis that family helped to build. Adam Todd, second, married Margaret Dodge, daughter of Jeremiah and Margaret Vanderbilt Dodge. The wife of John Jacob Astor, colonist, was Sarah Todd. They were married about the year 1785. Their son William married Margaret Armstrong. Vincent Astor is the fifth generation from John Jacob Astor and Sarah Todd Astor.

Timothy Todd of Vermont, a surgeon, was at the

battle of Bennington and a member of the Governor's council.

Ebcn Todd served through the War of the Revolution.

Thomas Todd was also a member of the Continental army. His son Charles was one of General Harrison's four aides and was afterwards minister to the Russian court.

In the War of 1812 George Todd was a lieutenant-colonel. His son David was governor of Ohio.

John Todd of Vermont was a preacher, author and educator. His *Students' Manual* had a great vogue, and he helped to found Mt. Holyoke Seminary.

The Todds patented lands in Gloucester county, Virginia, in 1652, and "Toddsbury Manor" was their home. Thomas Todd was the builder of Toddsbury House in 1658—and by his will it passed to his son Thomas. The house, built of brick, and the brick wall around the garden show extreme age. It is beautifully paneled on the inside. For generations it was the home of the Todds, who were noted for their lavish hospitality. There were a Christopher Todd and a Francis Todd in this family, as the tombstones show.

Thomas Todd was not only justice of Gloucester county, but he held other offices.

From Virginia and Pennsylvania some of the Todds came to Kentucky.

Mary Todd's ancestry traces back to Scottish Covenanters who, loving honor above worldly possessions and holding their faith greater than life, stubbornly fought the King and defied the established Church of England. Of the Covenanters captured at Bothwell Bridge and sentenced to transportation to America, two hundred were drowned in a shipwreck off the Orkneys. Among those who died thus were two of the Todds, Robert of Fenwick and James of Dunbar. In the same year, 1679, in which these two were drowned, John Todd, their brother, fled from the persecutions of Claverhouse in Scotland to find refuge in the north of Ireland. He is described as "Scottish laird," meaning simply that he owned land in fee simple and was a landlord, not that he was in any degree allied with the nobility. Two of his grandsons, Andrew and Robert Todd, came to America with their families in 1737 and located in Montgomery county, Pennsylvania. Robert Todd, born in Ireland in 1697, there married his first wife, Jean Smith. There were two sons of this marriage, David and John. David, born in Ireland, April 8, 1723, married Hannah Owen. Their third son, Levi Todd, married Jane, or Jean, Briggs. Their seventh child, Robert Smith Todd, married Eliza Ann

Parker. Their fourth child, Mary Todd, married Abraham Lincoln.

The genealogy of Mary Todd's mother, Eliza Ann Parker, traces back to the same Robert Todd, born in Ireland in 1697, the grandson of the John Todd, who fled from Scotland in 1679. Robert Todd's second wife was Isabella Bodley. Their second daughter, Elizabeth Todd, married William Parker. Their daughter, Elizabeth Parker, married General Andrew Porter. Their daughter, Elizabeth Porter, married her cousin, Major Robert Parker. Their fourth daughter, Eliza Ann Parker, married Robert Smith Todd. Their fourth child, Mary Todd, married Abraham Lincoln. It will be seen that Mary Todd's mother and father had the same great-grandfather, Robert Smith Todd having descended through his great-grandfather's first marriage to Jean Smith, and Eliza Ann Parker having descended through their mutual great-grandfather's second marriage to Isabella Bodley.

Mary Todd was related to many illustrious families in Pennsylvania: the Parkers, the Bodleys, Owens, McFarlands, Findlays, Majors, Porters. Her great-grandfather, General Andrew Porter, was the close friend of Washington. The Porters furnished Pennsylvania with a governor, and two of them filled cabinet positions. The Todds occupied positions of trust and honor and made the best of citizens wherever found.

"The Todds have intermarried with the Wickliffs, the Shelbys, the Breckenridges, the Didlakes, the Brents, the Woodleys, the Craigs, the Swifts, the McDowells, the Parkers, and so on and on. These families have intermarried with the Prestons, the McCaws, the Paynes, the Kinkeads, the Woolfolks, so the interests of the Todds extend to most houses in this community." (Lexington *Herald*, February 7, 1908.)

John Todd (Mary Todd's great-uncle), the brother of David Todd, was graduated at Princeton in 1749 and located in Louisa county, Virginia. He became so distinguished as a Presbyterian minister that it is said no history of the Presbyterian Church could be written without honorable mention of him. He was largely instrumental in establishing Transylvania Seminary (later Transylvania University), of Kentucky, and a gift of books from him formed the nucleus of the present fine library of the university.

David Todd, John Todd's brother, and the great-grandfather of Mary Todd, in 1783 sold his land in Pennsylvania for $12,000 and moved to Kentucky, he and his wife Hannah Owen being so grieved at the loss of their distinguished son, Colonel John Todd, who had been killed two years before at the battle of Blue

Licks (said to have been the bloodiest battle between the whites and Indians ever fought on Kentucky soil), that they wished to be with their remaining sons, Robert and Levi. David died the year after he moved to Kentucky. David Todd and Hannah Owen had four sons, one of whom, Owen, settled in Ohio and bore a brave part in Indian warfare. The other three, John, Robert, and Levi, were educated in a classical school in Virginia taught by their uncle, the Reverend John Todd. The eldest, Colonel John Todd, studied law and was appointed by Patrick Henry to be the first civil governor and lieutenant-commander of what is now the great State of Illinois. His record- or minute-book is now in the possession of the Chicago Historical Society and forms an interesting chapter in the history of that State.

During the War of the Revolution, General George Rogers Clark numbered among his brave soldiers, three of the Todd brothers.

In 1780 Kentucky was divided into three counties, Lincoln, Jefferson, and Fayette, and Thomas Jefferson, then governor of Virginia, appointed Colonel John Todd, colonel of Fayette county, Daniel Boone, as lieutenant, and Colonel Thomas Marshall, as Surveyor.

Robert, second son of David Todd and Hannah Owen, married his cousin, a daughter of Parson John

Todd, studied law and settled in Virginia. Levi, third son of David Todd and Hannah Owen, was born in Pennsylvania in 1756, was educated by his uncle, Parson John Todd, also studied law, and came early to Kentucky. He was purchaser of the first sale of lots in Lexington, Kentucky, in 1781, filled several offices of trust, became a brigadier- and then a major-general, both of which titles were won in actual service. He was a sensible, intelligent, well-educated man;

"a solid, substantial and enterprising citizen; a consistent Presbyterian, a valuable and faithful public servant; a good soldier and greatly respected when such qualities meant so much to the building of a state." (T. M. Green.)

General Levi Todd and Jane Briggs had eleven children. The seventh child, Robert Smith Todd (Mrs. Lincoln's father), was born February 25, 1791, in the house built by his father a few miles from Lexington on the Richmond Pike. He named the place "Ellersly" in honor of a small Scottish village once the home of the Todds. The house is still standing and is now owned by the Lexington Water Company.

Robert Smith Todd held positions of trust and responsibility. He was for many years clerk of the House of Representatives, was State senator and was the president of the Lexington branch of the Bank of Kentucky from its establishment in 1836 until his death.

"Not a man of brilliant talents, but one of clear strong mind, sound judgment, exemplary life and conduct, dignified and manly bearing, an influential and useful citizen." (T. M. Green, *Historic Families of Kentucky*.)

He and Eliza Ann Parker were married at the home of her parents in Short Street, Lexington, Kentucky. The property is now used as a Baptist orphans' home. The young couple went to housekeeping in a house built by Mr. Todd on an adjoining lot to the Parker home. They had seven children: Levi; Elizabeth; Frances; Mary (born, December 13, 1818); Ann; Robert Parker Todd, who died when he was fourteen months old and was buried in a cemetery on Main Street. The body of this child and that of his mother who had died when George was born were later removed and buried together in the Todd lot in the Lexington cemetery.

Mr. Todd had by his second marriage nine children: Robert Smith Todd, who lived only a few days; Samuel, killed in Confederate ranks at Shiloh; David, died from the effect of wounds received at Vicksburg— Confederate; Alexander, Confederate, killed at Baton Rouge; Margaret (Mrs. Kellogg); Martha (Mrs. White); Emilie (Mrs. Ben Hardin Helm); Elodie (Mrs. Dawson); and Katherine (Mrs. Herr).

CHAPTER III

A BLUE GRASS LASSIE

AFTER the death of Mr. Todd's first wife in July, 1825, and shortly after his second marriage, less than two years later, wishing to indulge his bride and himself in their passion for flowers, he bought a commodious double brick house with a wide hall in the center. On the grounds at the back were stables and servants' quarters, and best of all, in fact, the chief inducement in buying this place, was a large formal flower garden beautifully planned and filled with bulbs and flowering shrubs.

A conservatory at the left of the house opened from the library and led into the wide garden walk. A small stream which meandered through the lower end of the place, and in which the Todd youngsters waded and seined for minnows in and out of season, gave them much pleasure—in season, and out of season was the cause of many spankings when their wet clothes and croupy voices betrayed them. The Todd boys called this source of joy and sorrow the "blabbing brook." This stream has long since gone dry, the garden has been cut into building lots, and the house, though still

16

standing on Main Street in Lexington, Kentucky, has fallen sadly from its once desirable estate.

Mary Todd was eight years old when her father took, for his second bride, Miss Elizabeth Humphreys (daughter of Dr. Alexander Humphreys of Staunton, Virginia). Mrs. Todd's ancestry boasted men and women of scholarly attainments and high ideals. She often repeated the familiar saying, and believed it, too, that it took seven generations to make a lady.

Very calmly and competently she undertook the care and training of the six stepchildren, ranging in age from eighteen months to fourteen years.

Elizabeth at fourteen had already engaged in a romance with Ninian Wirt Edwards, a student at Transylvania University, and at about sixteen she married him and went to Springfield, Illinois, to preside over the governor's mansion, her father-in-law, Governor Ninian Edwards, being a widower.

Mary's grandmother, Mrs. Parker, bitterly resented the coming of a stepmother for her grandchildren, and never became reconciled with the second Mrs. Todd. Whether she influenced Mary, I do not know, but Mary was a bundle of nervous activity, wilful and original in planning mischief, and so the inevitable clashes with her very conventional young stepmother. However, in later years they became very good friends as they had many tastes in common. They both loved people, flowers, and books. The Todd library was well stocked with many standard works.

Mr. and Mrs. Todd were social favorites and they entertained in the lavish way then in vogue among their friends.

As far back as 1816, Lexington was considered the leading city of fashion in the West. A visitor at that time said:

"Lexington is as large as Cincinnati. The inhabitants are as polished and, I regret to add, as luxurious as those of Boston, New York or Baltimore, and their assemblies and parties are conducted with as much ease and grace as in the oldest towns in the Union."

Such a number of carriages filled the streets that a writer gave it the name of "The city that goes on wheels." In other and more solid respects Lexington was also quite exceptional: the literary culture and educational advantages had become such that in 1824 the city was spoken of far and wide as the "Athens of the West." Able and eloquent men filled the city's pulpits. Transylvania University had attained professors of European celebrity, and the town was filled to overflowing with academical, medical, and law students drawn from all over the Middle West and South. The local newspapers were leaders of the State press, and the

Lexington bar was probably the strongest in the United States.

Mrs. Todd's niece, Elizabeth Humphreys (afterwards married to Judge Norris of Batavia, Ohio) came to live in Mr. Todd's home to enjoy the superior advantages of the Lexington schools. Mary Todd and Elizabeth Humphreys became the most intimate and devoted of friends. They shared the same room, had the same friends and the same interests. They strolled, arms around each other, in the garden, sometimes read and studied there, breathing luxuriously the perfume of the lilac hedge and the arbor of roses, fragrant whiffs of spicy buster-pinks, heliotrope and lemon-verbena wafted from the borders.

Sometimes Mary, bubbling over with fun, would plan some prank to be played next day with Elizabeth's enthusiastic connivance. Mammy (the negro nurse) was suspicious of these moods in the children and would say "The debil been whisperin' 'round 'mong these chil'en." Then it was that she tasted her coffee with misgiving, expecting to find it salted or peppered. When summoned from the garden to supper, Mary and Elizabeth would have a rose tucked coquettishly over one ear, "for [Elizabeth wrote] Mary even as a child always loved to wear flowers in her hair. One spring morning, hearing the peep of a little turkey, Mary and

I flew out to the garden to find the little fellow. After hunting for some time we discovered the sound came from the honeysuckle vines which covered the latticed summer house at the end of the garden walk, the gentle little peep suddenly turned to the harsh note of the jay bird, and we saw the quick flicker of white in the wing of that masquerader, the mocking bird. The little rascal never tired of pretending to be some other feathered creature, now a field lark, now a cardinal, now the gentle peep of a little turkey. We had hunted half an hour for that little turkey."

Another day, there was great excitement over the expanding of a bud of the night-blooming cereus. Messengers were dispatched in every direction with notes inviting friends to witness the opening of this rare flower. It was said to bloom only once in a hundred years. The children, who for this occasion were allowed to remain out of bed until twelve o'clock, looked on in awed silence, while the delicate white petals slowly uncurled.

Mary and Elizabeth were very studious. With intent little faces they pored over their books every night, one on each side of a study table, a candle flickering between them. Now and then one or the other would stop long enough to pinch off with the snuffers a piece of the charred wick for a steadier light.

"Mary [Elizabeth wrote afterwards] was far in advance over girls of her age in education; she had a retentive memory and a mind that enabled her to grasp and thoroughly understand the lesson she was required to learn. Ours was a hard task, but long before I was through mine she had finished hers and was plying her knitting needles. We were required to knit ten rounds of sock every evening."

Mary was a pupil of the celebrated Mr. Ward, a man of unusual ability as an educator, also a regular martinet. His requirements and rules were very strict and woe to her who did not conform to the letter. Mary accepted the conditions cheerfully, even eagerly, and never came under his censure. Mr. Ward required his pupils to recite some of their lessons before breakfast. On bright summer mornings this was no hardship and Mary skipped blithely to her recitations, but she never murmured if conditions were not so pleasant, and when she had to get up out of her warm bed and dress by candle light, she and Elizabeth smiled and trudged sturdily through snow and sleet to school which was several city blocks from their home. Mary and Elizabeth had many good times together despite the fact that children were allowed but few privileges. Sunday school was a demure recreation, but looked forward to with pleasure as an opportunity to recite glibly, and a little more accurately than some other child, the Shorter Catechism.

Christmas was a time of great joy, and on Christmas day the children, who had sprung early out of bed to empty mother's long stockings, borrowed for the occasion to give Santa Claus more room in which to store their few and simple toys, were allowed to run around to their young friends in the neighborhood to wish "Happy Christmas" and "catch" them by screaming "Christmas gift" first out of excited lips. There was always church followed by a big Christmas dinner, a house full of company, and freedom from school tasks for a few days, so they were happy and satisfied.

Elizabeth writes to Mrs. Ben Hardin Helm (Mary's sister) :

"I love to think of the years I spent in your father's home. He was a man of unfailing courtesy and was remarkably kind to me. It was a charming home. Some very distinguished men came to Lexington in those days, and many of them were entertained at your father's home. Aunt was very delicate and I often wonder how she lived through some of those years.

"Jane Sanders, a negro slave, was a treasure. She was brought up and trained by Aunt's mother. She was our stand-by, especially as some of the other slaves were very trifling. Old Chaney was a delightful cook but very cross and ill-tempered.   Nelson, next to Jane in dependability, serving very well in the dining room. He did the marketing and was a good financier as he managed to save enough out of the market money to buy himself a horse.   Sally was a jewel of a black mammy. She alternately spoiled and scolded the children, but they loved her and never rebelled against her authority.   Dear Old Mammy Sally was very pious and loved to go to the 'white folks' church and sit in the gallery reserved for negroes, she took turn about in church-going with Judy (a young assistant nurse owned by Mrs. Todd's mother) though the latter had decidedly the advantage in that regard, as Mammy would never trust a sick child or very young baby to Judy—Judy, who was so good, and reliable, and versatile that all of us called on her for everything—but Mammy was very zealous and no less jealous in her care of 'my chil'en' as she called the little Todds.

"Mammy never seemed to come home from church in a very good humor and always chided Judy for some fancied neglect of the children.   We also came in for our share of the scolding.   Such occasions afforded Mammy a fine opportunity to preach the gospel to us with impassioned oratory and great dramatic effect, and our youthful escapades called down upon our devoted heads such dire punishments in the future that we shivered with half-believing fear and stopped our ears with our fingers. Mary was so fascinated with Mammy's description of his Satanic majesty that she made her repeat it time and time again, although we knew it by heart. We realized, of course, that Mammy mixed the Scriptures with many inappropriate proverbs and sayings which salved our fear of future torment. 'Mammy,' Mary would innocently ask, taking her fingers out of her ears, 'do you think you could have dreamed that about the old bad man? I am sure I saw you nod in church.' Mammy would bridle indignantly. 'Chile, you never saw me do no such ill mannered doin's.' Mary would glance mischievously at me, 'Mammy, didn't you say he has horns?' 'Yes, honey,' would answer Mammy, 'just like that old male cow animal out at your Uncle Stuart's house in the country, and ole man Satan bellers and shakes his head and sharpens up his horns on the ground and paws up the dust with both his front feet at once.' 'But,' would interrupt Mary, 'what does he stand on when he is pawing with both feet? Has he four legs?' 'No, honey,' Mammy would patiently explain, 'but he can stand on his tail and that makes him mo' fearsome like.' 'I don't think his tail is the color you say it is,' would prod Mary. 'It would naturally be black.' 'No, chile,' emphatically from Mammy, 'you must not de-

moralize the holy word which I heared out'en the
preacher's own mouth, right at your pa's dinner table.'
With the solemn voice and manner she always used
when she thought she was quoting the gospel truth,
straight out of the Bible, she would intone 'Neat but
not gaudy as the debil said when he painted his tail pea
green.' Here was the delicious point in the story,
where Mary always bubbled over with laughter and
the scandalized old nurse would say indignantly,
'Well, I hopes and prays you won't never have to see
his old green tail,' but as if doubting the description
herself she would add 'Course the old rapscallion might
have told a lie about the color he painted his tail, it
wouldn't a been past him to try to fool poor humans
who would just naturally think his tail would be black.'

"Mammy was convinced that the jay birds went to
hell every Friday night and told the devil all of our
shortcomings of the previous week. Mary was the
only one of us brave enough to challenge Satan's messenger. The little rascal with his crested head tilted
sidewise looked so impudent that Mary could not resist retaliation. She chanted:

" 'Howdy, Mr. Jay. You are a tell-tale-tell.
    You play the spy each day, then carry tales to hell.'

"After which poetic effusion, the bird answering rau-

cously 'Jay! jay!' Mary ran shrieking to Mammy for
protection. Mammy described the visit of 'Mr. Jay'
to the 'bad place' in this wise:

" 'They's a tall table on one side of the room an' a
little debil settin' up on a stool so high that his tail
don't no way tech the flo'. Mr. Jay twitters in ole man
Satan's ears: "Mary hid Mammy's slippers when po'
old Mammy was tryin' to res' her foots in the garden
after lopin' 'roun' all day after bad chil'en." Old Man
Satan bellers: "Write that down in yo' big book, little
son." Mr. Jay: "Lis'beth he'ps Mary in all her mis-
*chee*vous doin's." Old Man Satan: "Write that down
son, keerful—don't trus' nary thing to yo' recomenem-
brance." Mr. Jay: "Ann hollered when Mammy
curled her hair." ' And so on to the end of the grievous
history of seven long days filled with the iniquities of
the little Todds.

"Mammy had a retentive memory and at each ar-
raignment she would fix a stern, accusing eye on the
culprit who with a stricken look would nod her head
in shamed acquiescence to the count against her."

Elizabeth says she never but once saw Mary exhibit
temper. When she was ten years old the little girl
became fascinated by the lovely bouffant summer
dresses that puffed and swayed so entrancingly on the
hoop-skirted ladies of the period. She felt that she

simply must have a swaying, swishing skirt of her own. She looked in great disdain at her plain gingham school dresses and simple white muslin frocks for Sunday. Her longing grew apace. She instinctively knew that her request for a hoop skirt would be considered pre-posterous, would be refused; but she must have one and be in the admired fashion. It was a terrible worry and caused a great amount of planning and thinking. At last her nimble wits found a way and she told Elizabeth of her plan—she would go to Mrs. Hostetter's and ask her for some of her weeping willow branches and she and Elizabeth would make hoop skirts and wear them to Sunday school the following morning. So at a convenient time one Saturday afternoon, she got her little pink sunbonnet, found a basket, and slipped off. She was gone a long time, but when she came back she was abundantly supplied with the precious willows which she triumphantly showed Elizabeth and which they carefully hid in a closet in their bedroom.

They were afraid to begin their preparations until after supper. With mysterious nods and glances the little conspirators waited impatiently, fearing mightily some interruption of their plan, but at last the time was ripe. They took a candle, went to their room and locked the door, took out of the closet the basket of willow switches and their narrow little white muslin frocks and, seated on the floor, lost no time in commencing the important work before them. Their progress was awkward and slow and they were surprised and startled when Mrs. Todd on her way to her bedroom tapped on the door and told them it was time they were in bed. Mary answered, "Yes, mother," and she and Elizabeth waited as quietly as mice until they thought everybody must be asleep; then relighting their candle they worked nearly all night.

At last, with a thrill of delight, they viewed their finished handiwork and proudly hung the hoop-skirted dresses in the closet. They were too excited to sleep, so it was easy to get down to breakfast in good time. As soon as they could they flew upstairs and hurriedly dressed. Mary, with a buoyant vitality in all her movements, was dressed first, and out on the street, before Elizabeth had reached the front door. One moment and they would have been safe, but, alas, as fate would have it, Mrs. Todd coming into the hall at that moment gave one amazed glance at Elizabeth. She reached the door in a second and called Mary back. "There we stood before her," said Elizabeth, many years later, "a burlesque on vanity, two of the most grotesque figures her eyes ever fell upon, with hoops that bulged in the front and at the back, while they fell in at the sides," the narrow white muslin skirts stretched to the bursting point. The children had sewed in the willow branches just as they came off the tree, one end being large and rather stiff, and the other end tapering to a flexible tip.

Mrs. Todd looked them over from head to foot with great amusement and laughed.

"What frights you are. Take those awful things off, dress yourselves properly and go to Sunday school." The two little girls, their plans all awry, their precious hoop skirts ridiculed, went to their room chagrined and mortified, and Mary burst into a flood of angry tears. She thought they were badly treated and freely said so. Her cherished plan came to naught, her world for the moment in ruins. Elizabeth agreed most heartily with everything Mary said but, being the guest of her aunt, said nothing:

"It is well," she wrote long afterwards, "that our display was confined to our own premises. If we had got into the McChord Church, which we were so anxious to do, Mr. Young's eloquent flights of oratory would have fallen on deaf ears and he as well as the congregation would have been convulsed with laughter and Aunt too mortified to hold up her head. This escapade was a standing joke in the family for years. A fine opportunity for the gleeful teasing of the boys, who, witlessly we thought, presented us with switches, making grand flourishing bows and low and insulting suggestions as to how the switches should be applied.

"Our feelings were somewhat salved when your father soon after came up from New Orleans, bringing each of us some lovely, sheer, embroidered pink muslin. Much to Mary's delight, Aunt allowed her to direct the sewing woman how to make the frocks. Your father, also on that trip, brought us each a doll which squeaked most entrancingly when pressed on its little stomach. We thought the squeak sounded like 'Mama' and we hugged our babies with love and pride. We made them clothes, clumsily put together. Mary afterwards developed a real talent for sewing and used her needle with artistic effect. Aunt had never learned to sew, and Mary was the only one of the family of girls who ever learned to use her needle with skill. Aunt did not, however, idly fold her hands; whenever she was not holding a book she was knitting or crocheting, and all of us were taught to knit."

Among Mary's most intimate friends at this time were her cousins, Margaret and Mary Wickliffe. Margaret married General William Preston, and Mary married Colonel John Preston. Mary Jane Warfield was another friend. Elizabeth Todd (Mrs. Ninian Edwards) acted as bridesmaid when Mary Jane Warfield became Mrs. Cassius M. Clay. Another intimate

friend and schoolmate was Miss Bodley, afterwards
Mrs. Owsley of Louisville, Kentucky. Perhaps her
most intimate friend, outside of Elizabeth Humphreys,
was her cousin Margaret Stuart (Mrs. Woodrow), sister of the Honorable John Todd Stuart of Springfield,
Illinois. The father of these two was the Reverend
Robert Stuart (he had married Robert Smith Todd's
sister). The Reverend Robert Stuart, one of the first
three professors of Transylvania University (lan-
guages), was minister of a noted Presbyterian church
at Walnut Hills, a few miles out of Lexington, where
he had his country home.

The Todds and Stuarts were very intimate and there
was much visiting between the two families. In the
summer and autumn there were many picnics in the
woods, and the big family of boys and girls hunted
walnuts and chestnuts and played games and shouted
with the sheer joy of just being alive.

Mary in those days was called a "tomboy," was always playing pranks, and was the fearless and inventive
leader in every possible kind of mischief.

In the winter when the Todd children were allowed
to spend the week-end at their uncle's country place,
there were sleigh rides in the farm wagons put on run-
ners and filled with straw, and in the evenings before
the big, glowing, open fireplace with its huge back log

and showers of sparks flying up the wide chimney, there were apples to be roasted and corn to be popped and long interesting talks, conundrums to guess, and recitations of poems by Mary.

Mrs. Woodrow wrote: "Mary's love for poetry, which she was forever reciting, was the cause of many a jest among her friends. Page after page of classic poetry she could recite and liked nothing better. She was very highly strung, nervous, impulsive, excitable, having an emotional temperament much like an April day, sunning all over with laughter one moment, the next crying as though her heart would break."

Mary had an aunt living at Walnut Hills, her father's sister married to Charles Carr. A number of children were spending the day with her at her country place when a band of friendly Indians passed. All of these children had been brought up on gruesome tales of marauding and murderous bands of Indians. Not one of them but had heard of some ancestor who had been tomahawked and scalped. Mary had heard her uncle, John Todd, tell of the time he had been compelled to run the gauntlet and how he had miraculously escaped. Another of her father's brothers had been captured by the Indians and was held by them for three years before he found an opportunity to evade their vigilance; so no wonder, when glancing out of the window and seeing this band of redskins approaching bedecked in blankets and feathers, the children wildly scampered in every direction trying to find places to hide. Mary ran to the great open fireplace before which was a fire screen and crept behind it, but this seemed too big a place for such a little slender body, so she dashed out to seek another hiding place. The Indians were closer. All the other children were safely hidden. She had lost valuable time, her only hope was heaven, so in a panic, but with a beautiful faith, she stood in the center of the room and cried "Hide me, oh, my Savior, hide." This same faith was, later in life, her chief source of help and comfort, when most other sources failed her.

One day the latter part of June, 1828, Mary and Elizabeth in their little strapped slippers climbed the three folding steps of the big lumbering Todd carriage which was to convey them the twenty-six miles over to Frankfort. The journey would consume nearly four hours, as the big carriage horses trotted very sedately. The two little girls in their white organdy frocks and blue satin sashes looked, for all the world, as if they had intended to be a part of nature's color scheme, for even the wild roses which sprawled over the stone fences along the Frankfort pike were duplicated in the wreaths of pink roses which circled their wide-brimmed, flapping, leghorn hats. They were on their way to spend a happy week with Mrs. Alexander Humphreys, Mrs. Todd's mother—Elizabeth's own grandmother, and Mary's step-grandmother. Mrs. Humphreys was a highly educated old lady who, naughtily for her day and generation, read Voltaire in French. She also doted on Volney, both books being by her much bracketed and interlined. Mrs. Humphreys' four brothers all attained eminence. Preston Brown was a skillful physician; John Brown served as the first United States senator from Kentucky; James Brown was twice elected to the United States Senate from Louisiana and later became minister to France. Dr. Samuel Brown was the earliest professor of medicine in Transylvania and the most famous physician of his day in the West. After his graduation from college he spent ten years studying medicine in Edinburgh. He was especially noted as being the first to introduce vaccination into this country. Dr. Samuel Brown was particularly fond of his niece, Mrs. Robert S. Todd, and the massive silver used each day on the Todd table was his wedding gift to her. Mrs. Humphreys was an "exquisite" in dress and mind and manner, the quintessence of all the elegance, virtue, and culture which Mary hoped to emulate. She said to Elizabeth Humphreys, "If I can only be, when I am grown up, just like Grandmother Humphreys, I will be perfectly satisfied with myself."

Mary and Elizabeth were allowed to go to a ball in Frankfort with their grandmother who at the age of seventy-three, in satin gown and imported lace cap from France, led the grand march. Both children had a romantic attachment for this charming old lady, who was an emancipationist and had great influence in forming Mary's views on that subject. She died when Mary was eighteen, and in her will of twenty-four paragraphs, eight of them direct the disposition of slaves.

In the name of God Amen: I, Mary Humphreys, of the town of South Frankfort, and County of Franklin and State of Kentucky, do make and ordain this my last will and testament . . .

9th. I devise my negro slave, John Wales, unto my son, David C. Humphreys, until the Twenty-fifth day of December, Eighteen Hundred and Forty, on which said day the said John Wales is to be free and emancipate from all kind of servitude.

10th. I devise my negro girl, Jane, to my daughter, Elizabeth Todd, until the twenty-fifth day of December, Eighteen Hundred and Forty-four, on which said date the said Jane is to be free from all kind of servi-

tude and should the said Jane have any children before
the day on which she is to be free, the said child or
children if boys are hereby devised to the said Elizabeth L. Todd until they respectively attain the age of
twenty-eight years, whereby they are to be free and
emancipate from all manner of servitude, if girls they
are hereby devised to the said Elizabeth L. Todd until
they respectively attain the age of twenty-one years,
when they and any increase they may have are to be
free and emancipate from all manner of servitude.

11th. It is my will and desire that my negro man
slave (name blotted) be free and emancipate from all
kind of servitude on the twenty-eighth day of December, Eighteen Hundred and Forty-one.

12th. It is my will and desire that my negro boy,
Abraham, be free and emancipate from all kind of
servitude on the Twenty-fifth day of December, Eighteen Hundred and Forty-six.

13th. It is my will and desire that my negro boy, Al-
fred, be free and emancipate from all kinds of servitude
on the Twenty —— day of December, Eighteen Hundred and Fifty-two.

14th. It is my desire that my negro woman, Judy,
be free and emancipate from all kind of servitude on
the Twenty-fifth day of December, Eighteen Hundred
and Thirty-nine. If before that time she has any

children, the said increase of males are to be —— until they are respectively twenty-eight years of age, and as they respectively attain that age, they are to be free and emancipate from all kind of servitude, the said increase of females are to serve until they are respectively twenty-one years old, and as they respectively attain that age, they and any increase they may have are to be free and emancipate from all kind of servitude.

15th. It is my will and desire that my negro woman, ——, be free and emancipate from all kind of servitude on the Twenty-fifth day of December, Eighteen Hundred and Forty-two. If before that time she has any children, the said increase of males are to serve until they are respectively twenty-eight years old and as they respectively attain that age, they are to be free and emancipate from all kind of servitude, the said increase of females are to serve until they are respectively twenty-one years old and as they respectively attain that age, they and any increase they may have are to be free and emancipate from all kind of servitude.

16th. It is my will and desire that my negro girl, Mary Jane, be free and emancipate from all kind of servitude on the Twenty-fifth day of December, Eighteen Hundred and Fifty-five, if before that time she has any increase, the said increase of males are to serve until they are respectively twenty-eight years old and as they respectively attain that age they are to be free and emancipate from all kind of servitude, the said increase of females are to serve until they are respectively twenty-one years old and as they respectively attain that age they and any increase they may have are to be free and emancipate from all kind of servitude whatever.

17th. It is my will and desire that my executor hire out —— all of the above slaves (except John Wales and Jane) and their increase until the periods respectively arrive at which they are to be free and I further authorize and empower my said executor to make any contract he may think proper with the said slaves, or their increase for the purchase by them of the time that they, or their increase may have to serve.

Mary and Elizabeth shivered with horror over a revolting occurrence in New Orleans. The newspapers North and South were filled with accounts of it, and of the riots afterwards which popular indignation instigated. The house of Mr. and Mrs. Lalaurie being discovered in flames, the doors were broken open and several unfortunate slaves were discovered chained in the attic! They were removed to a place of safety where they would be protected from the cruelty of their owners.

Says the *Bee* of April 11, 1834: "The populace have repaired to the scene of this cruelty and have destroyed everything upon which they could lay their hands. At the time of inditing this it was found necessary, for the purpose of restoring order, for the sheriff and his officers to repair to the place of riot and to interpose the authority of the state. . . . Nearly the whole of the edifice is demolished, scarcely anything remains but the walls which the popular vengeance have ornamented with inscriptions far from complimentary to its late occupants."

The story goes that the Lalauries barely escaped with their lives, and never dared show their faces in New Orleans again.

Elizabeth Humphreys (Mrs. Norris), writing to Mrs. Ben Hardin Helm: "We were horrified and talked of nothing else for days. If one such case could happen, it damned the whole institution, though in our own family, I think the slaves rather managed us, and we heard of no cruelty to the slaves of our friends who seemed to love and trust their servants as we did ours. Grandmother Humphreys was freeing her slaves, the women at twenty-one, the men at twenty-eight. Mary and I wondered if Mammy wanted to be free; we concluded she did not. How could we do without Mammy, and how could she exist without us? It would just about kill her to give up bossing her white 'chillun.' She was part, and a very important, loved and venerated part, of our family. We heard a knocking one night. Mary, who was reading, was very much annoyed.

" 'Mammy,' she cried impatiently, 'what is that knocking? It disturbs me so I can't read.'

" 'That,' said Mammy, whispering mysteriously, 'might be a run-a-way nigger. We have a mark on the fence—I made it myself—to show that if any run-a-way is hongry he can get vittles right here. All of 'em knows the sign, I have fed many a one.' 'Oh,' cried Mary, springing up, 'you know, Mammy, it is against the law to help run-a-way slaves, but I will go down and give him food myself.' 'No, honey,' cried Mammy, restraining her, 'he would hide from you like a scared rabbit, nothing but a black hand reaching out to him can give that nigger cornbread and bacon.'

"We kept Mammy's secret," continued Elizabeth, "and though we often listened, did not again hear the knocking; but from that time our ears were keyed for any tales of oppression. Even our pampered slaves may have grumbled among themselves; one day when we were all out in the county at Buena Vista (Mrs. Todd's country place) Aunt called little Dick, seven or eight years old and black as the ace of spades. 'Dick,'

she said, when the little fellow reluctantly left off playing with the white children, 'run down to the spring
and get Miss Betsy a pitcher of fresh water.' The
spring, of very fine, sparkling, ice-cold water, being
only a stone's throw from the house, and the pitcher
holding only a quart, all of us laughed heartily as we
heard the little rascal mutter, intending that we should
hear him, 'The white folks just works me to death.' It
made no impression on me at the time but I have wondered since if some of the older slaves' 'being worked
to death' was like little Dick's grumbling."

Mary when fourteen years of age was a violent little
Whig. Almost from her babyhood at her father's table
—when still in short dresses and curls tied with ribbons,
she had been allowed to come in at the end of dinner
for dessert—she had heard politics discussed by eminent men who had patted her on the head and who
sometimes, much to Mary's delight, gallantly kissed her
hand. She stood in no awe of great men, they were
to her as much a matter of course as the air she breathed.
Moreover, at fourteen she knew why she was a Whig
and not a Democrat. General Andrew Jackson was a
Democrat, and she hated him with all her might and
main because he was a candidate for reëlection to the
Presidency against her dear friend, Mr. Henry Clay.
On Saturday, September 29, 1832, Lexington was boil-

ing with excitement. General Jackson was coming! The streets were crowded with people from all over the State. Men in broadcloth rubbed elbows with men in jeans, city women in bright filmy dresses filled handsome carriages, women from the rural districts crowded into rough wagons with all their children. All on tiptoe to take part in the excitement, no matter what their politics.

A big rally and barbecue had been planned by the Democrats in honor of the President of the United States, who was at the same time their chosen candidate for reëlection. The atmosphere at "Fowler's Garden" was permeated with the appetizing aroma of roast beef and roast pig; whisky in open buckets and kegs, great baskets of fried chicken, beaten biscuits, preserves, pickle, cakes, and pies were on their way to be piled on the long tables of rough boards stretched under the trees. All comers were welcome to this political feast.

"Old Hickory," in an open carriage, seated by the side of Governor Brethitt, who had lately been elected to that office by the Democrats, was escorted by an immense procession—military companies, clubs, orders, societies, bands of music, horsemen, men on foot bearing banners with political inscriptions surmounted by game cocks crowing so lustily as to be heard above the hubbub of music and shouts. Men were shouting, women were waving handkerchiefs and hickory twigs. Mary, viewing the procession from a carriage in the company of a little Democratic friend who was wildly clapping, said, "I wouldn't think of cheering General Jackson, for he is not our candidate, but he is not as ugly as I heard he was."

"Ugly!" exclaimed the little Democrat. "If you call General Jackson ugly, what do you think of Mr. Clay?"

"Mr. Henry Clay," said Mary coolly, "is the handsomest man in town and has the best manners of anybody—except my father," she added dutifully. "We are going to snow General Jackson under and freeze his long face so that he will never smile again."

"Humph!" retorted the little Democrat, "Andrew Jackson with his long face is better looking than Henry Clay and your father both rolled into one."

This was too much. And the disagreement between the two little politicians ended in an estrangement lasting through many years.

Elizabeth wrote:

"Mary and I could never pass the confectionery shop of Monsieur Giron. Most of our small allowance of pocket money went to swell his coffers, not so much for the pleasure of the palate as for the joy of filling our eyes with the beauty of his unique creations.

"When Aunt was arranging for a dining or a party we always begged to be allowed to take the written order to Monsieur that we might feast our eyes on the iced cakes decorated with garlands of pink sugar roses, or the bride's cakes with their fountains of clear, spun sugar pyramiding in the center, veiling tiny fat cupids or little sugar brides. This Frenchman was an artist in his line and his sweets shop was one of the features of Lexington. Above his shop he had a large and handsomely decorated ballroom; in this room many famous balls were given. Mary chatted to Monsieur in French, much to his delight."

It was at this time, when Mary was fourteen years old, that she entered the French boarding-school conducted by two charming French gentlewomen in a quaint, beautiful place, now Mentelle Park, in Lexington. She boarded there four years, coming home Friday evening and returning early Monday morning. Nothing but French was spoken in that school, and during the four years of her tuition she acquired a thorough knowledge of the language and spoke the purest Parisian. As long as she lived she read the finest French authors.

Monsieur and Madame Mentelle and their two daughters were French refugees who had fled from the fury of the bloodthirsty mobs at the beginning of the French Revolution. Loyal to their unfortunate sovereign Louis XVI, and loving with deep devotion the frivolous but gentle and brave Queen Marie Antoinette, they could never allude to these "martyrs" without tears. And the poor little Dauphin! At the thought of the brutal treatment that poor child received at the hands of his heartless captors, Monsieur Mentelle's face would flush a deep red and his hands would clench in impotent rage. Landing in America, the Mentelles made their way to Lexington, where the accomplished Madame Mentelle opened her famous and exclusive little school, the only school in Kentucky where French was the sole language spoken.

At sixteen Mary spoke French very fluently. A French play had been studied, and Mary was given the principal part.

"Indeed," wrote Elizabeth, "she was the star actress of the school, and I was thrilled with her talent. It was not like the first time I saw her in a small part when I was trembling with nervousness for fear she might forget her lines; this was quite an occasion, and each pupil was allowed to invite a guest. Of course, Mary invited me. I was to come early that Friday afternoon and bring a cake which was Mary's contribution to the refreshments to be served after the play. I had promised to bring a basket of flowers for the table, though

it was late for flowers and very hot and dusty that fall.
I thought Nelson would never bring the carriage
around to the door, but when it came at last, Mary
Jane [a young slave girl belonging to Mrs. Todd]
was seated inside with the big round hat box in which
Aunt Chaney had carefully placed the cake.

"Mary was waiting impatiently at the door as we
drove up, and flew at me like a whirlwind. I had not
seen her for a week and I thought she had grown pret-
tier during that time, she looked so dainty in her fresh
white muslin frock and silk sash! Her cheeks were
as pink as the tea roses I had gathered for her. I always thought of tea roses in connection with Mary, they
seemed so to suit her, to be a part of her. Her blue
eyes were sparkling with excitement, her pretty chestnut curls were bright and glossy. She chattered a volu-
ble welcome in French, not being allowed to speak a
word of English until she left Madame Mentelle's
premises. Mary Jane, who could not understand the
'outlandish talk,' shied off from Mary like a skittish
colt; she was holding tightly to the hat box until I took
it from her and told her to go and get Miss Mary's
things and put them in the carriage. Mary Jane hated
to go with me for Mary on Friday afternoons. I think
she was really superstitiously afraid of the unfamiliar
tongue.

"In the carriage on the way home Mary said, 'Monsieur Giron must have made that cake with his own hands.' 'No, ma'am,' exclaimed Mary Jane indignantly, 'Aunt Chaney made that cake her own self. Her hands is just as knowin' as that Frenchy's is.' 'That is enough,' said Mary smiling. 'It looked like Monsieur Giron; the icing on that cake was as white as Aunt Chaney is black and it was as light and fine grained inside as she is heavy and cross-grained outside. Bless her old heart, I am going to give her a bear's hug just as soon as I get home—if she will let me—I have not had a good scolding for a week but trust Aunt Chaney and Mammy to supply that lack.'

" 'You limb,' I laughed, 'you are aching for that scolding and I have no doubt you will soon deserve it. You are planning some mischief right now,' I challenged, 'I see it in your eyes.' 'Yes,' dimpled Mary, 'I am going to insist that Monsieur Giron made that cake; then, when Aunt Chaney flies into one of her fierce rages and bangs the pans and kettles and orders me out of her kitchen I am going to give her the red and yellow bandanna head handkerchief I bought for her and tell her that Monsieur Giron with all his icing and spicing could not make a cake half so "confectionery" as hers. Aunt Chaney will fairly eat me up for praising her cake so highly.' 'Then,' she continued, warming to her theme, 'I'll tell Mammy that I always did like biggoty Mr. Fox better than Br'er Rabbit and that I am sure the devil did not paint his tail pea green but a lovely sunshiny yellow and made of it a road leading down to the bad place. A primrose path of ease and dalliance, leading to abysmal depths of sin and sorrow. Won't Mammy just revel in that combination? It would not surprise me if she quotes it to the children as Holy Writ.'

"As we drove down Main Street busily chatting, I noticed an old white man shambling along the sidewalk. I had often seen him before on the streets of Lexington and smiled at his resemblance to a scarecrow. The old fellow boasted that he and Henry Clay were born in the same county in Virginia and that he and 'Henry' had played ball together when they were children. Mary suddenly ordered Nelson to stop. 'Old King Solomon!' she cried. 'Get out with me, Elizabeth, we must not pass him without shaking hands, and I know he needs a little piece of money for tobacco. I wish I could give him a cake of soap instead, if it would not insult him.' Nelson, who was scandalized at Miss Mary and Miss Lizzie getting out in the dust to shake hands with the grotesque, shambling old creature, muttered loud enough for us to to hear, 'Shaking hands with every old po' white trash dey meets on de road. I'm gwine to tell Miss Betsy quick as I get home.'

"Mary held her hand out to old Sol who took it gingerly. 'Howdy, Miss Mary, you ain't never too proud to speak to me.' 'Too proud to speak to you!' cried Mary. 'I am proud when you speak to me! I will never forget last summer when you were the bravest man in town, when you worked night and day digging, digging, digging the graves of those poor people who died like flies of the cholera. You dug the graves of some of my best friends.' Her eyes were brimming with tears. 'You were not afraid! You are a hero!'

"Old Sol listened with a furtive air of embarrassment tinged with indifference. His face brightened with interest, however, and he pulled at his disreputable old hat when Mary handed him the little piece of money for tobacco. When we were again seated in the carriage Mary said, 'I missed you terribly last summer, Elizabeth, but you were certainly lucky not to be in Lexington. I will never, never forget that terrible time. The choking fumes of the tar that mother made Nelson burn all through the house, the lime and whitewash over everything, the deadly quiet everywhere!

" 'When the baby cried it seemed as if it must be heard all over town. Nothing on the streets but the drivers and horses of the dead-carts piled with the bodies of those who had just died, the relatives of the dead being too frightened to make decent burial clothes, the poor bodies were wrapped in sheets and blankets, many of them just as they were dressed when the plague caught them. Toward the last not even coffins. Father had all the trunks and boxes taken out of the attic and hauled to "Cheapside" to be given to the people who could not get coffins. Other people did the same and still so very, very many had to be buried in trenches, just dumped in like old dead dogs.

" 'They would not let us eat fruit nor vegetables, just beaten biscuits, eggs, and boiled milk and boiled water and both always tepid. Elizabeth, I pledge you my word I was actually hungry. Oh, not for just food but for something different. You know how I like mulberries. I begged mother so hard she said I might eat just one—and I did—just one at a time, but the time rolled around every few minutes until Aunt Chaney caught me and then such a to do! Mother sent for the doctor posthaste, and Mammy made me take ipecac, the great emergency medicine in our family. Mammy almost had to hold my nose to make me take it.

" 'But what was worse than all, everybody was frightened half to death, talking in whispers, almost afraid to breathe, and poor, brave old Sol going along as if nothing terrible was happening, just doing everything he could. Oh, Elizabeth, I am so ashamed of myself! Just to think, two years ago I was laughing at him, laughing at his funny old clothes, laughing because he, a white man, had been publicly sold as a vagabond to an old negro woman for thirty cents. Oh, I was an unspeakable little beast,' wept Mary. 'I cannot forgive myself, but'—smiling at me through her tears—'it was a lucky bargain for the old darkey.

" 'Every evening Sol handed her his day's wages and, of course, she did it for Sol's own good, but she never handed him back enough to get on a real good spree,' and, pensively, 'That is the only time he is really happy, but think of the poor, ragged, brave old soul being sold to a negro! It's all wrong, Elizabeth!' she exclaimed with heat, 'this selling human beings into slavery; think of our selling cross old Aunt Chaney or Mammy or'—laying her hand affectionately on Mary Jane's knee, seated opposite,—'or foolish little Mary Jane, or any one of our servants. I love them all! It would break my heart. I would feel as if I were selling a member of my own family. Has grandmother [Mrs. Humphreys] heard from John yet? Since she freed him, educated him for the ministry and sent him to make Scotch Presbyterians of the heathen in Liberia, I think he ought to write very interesting letters home, but perhaps he is too busy teaching the Shorter Catechism to the cannibals in the jungles of Africa.—Goodness!' she exclaimed, her eyes widening at a gruesome thought, 'they eat each other down there, Elizabeth, I never thought of it before. Oh poor, poor John!'

"Mary was like this always, her mood changing with every new thought. Like the varying patterns made by each slight turn of a kaleidoscope, her face expressed her varying moods, with eyes half closed and looking through her long lashes she had the demure shyness of a little Quakeress, but presto! they now gleamed with mischief, and before you could be quite sure of that, her dimple was gone and her eyes were brimful of tears. How I hated to see her go back to school on Monday morning."

"Mary even as a school girl in her gingham dresses was certainly very pretty," said Elizabeth. "She had clear blue eyes, long lashes, light brown hair with a glint of bronze, and a lovely complexion. Her figure was beautiful and no Old Master ever modeled a more perfect arm and hand."

Many years ago a reporter on the Louisville *Courier-Journal* wrote:

"There is still living in Louisville an old lady who for four years was a fellow pupil of Mary Todd's at Madame Mentelle's school for young ladies, at that time the most exclusive establishment of the kind in the

"Ashland"

The home of Henry Clay near Lexington, Kentucky

"HELM PLACE"

The home of Mrs. Ben Hardin Helm (Emilie Todd), Mrs. Lincoln's sister, near Lexington, Kentucky

State of Kentucky. 'Mary Todd,' said this old lady, 'was one of the brightest girls in Madame Mentelle's school, always had the highest marks and took the biggest prizes. French was the language of the school and Mary spoke it as fluently as did Madame herself. . . . She was a merry, companionable girl with a smile for everybody. She was really the life of the school, always ready for a good time and willing to contribute even more than her own share in promoting it."

Elizabeth writes: "At different times French gentlemen came to the University to study English, and when one was fortunate enough to meet Mary, he was surprised and delighted to find her a fluent conversationalist in his own language. It was also at Madame Mentelle's that Mary learned to dance so gracefully. The class was not allowed to receive visitors, so to enliven the evenings Monsieur Mentelle would take his violin, while Madame Mentelle and her two accomplished daughters would take their pupils on the floor and respond to his music in the dance. In after years it remained her favorite amusement and the aristocratic society of Lexington afforded her ample opportunity for the indulgence of the pastime."

Mrs. Todd was delicate and the water of Crab Orchard Springs had been ordered by her doctor. A great many wealthy people from all over the State and from many parts of the South came with their entire families to Crab Orchard Springs in Kentucky. Mrs. Todd frequently met there the family of her brother, Alexander Humphreys of New Orleans, and her pretty nieces went home with her to stay in Kentucky until frost made it safe for them to return South.

The little Todds looked forward with greater excitement to their annual short stay at Crab Orchard Springs than the modern child would feel at the prospect of a trip to Europe. The bustle of preparation; the piles of fresh little muslin dresses; the carriages filled with children and babies and nurses, for only the older boys, who objected to going, were left at home; the long drive; the meeting with old friends and acquaintances; the new arrivals each day driving up in state with jingling harness and prancing horses; the finely dressed ladies stepping mincingly down the carriage steps in mortal dread of showing their ankles; the beaux flocking around to greet those they knew and perchance to gain a fleeting glimpse of those same carefully guarded ankles. The negro fiddlers, the candlelight flickering from innumerable sconces over the bright, filmy ball dresses of the belles, and the courtly bowing and scraping of the beaux.

Mary, after the marriage of Frances Todd was the

eldest of the Todd daughters left at home, and in Mary's appearance, in her wit, her savoir faire and exquisite manner; her graceful dancing, which even as a little schoolgirl made her a desirable partner, Mrs. Todd took a very pardonable pride, for since Mary was a romping "tomboy" of eight years she had trained her in all the social graces.

Mary was very vivacious and at eighteen she and Elizabeth were popular belles. They received their visitors in the parlor together. Said Elizabeth: "Among them were many scholarly, intellectual men; but Mary never at any time showed the least partiality for any one of them. Indeed, at times, her face indicated a decided lack of interest and she accepted their attention without enthusiasm. Without meaning to wound, she now and then could not restrain a witty, sarcastic speech that cut deeper than she intended, for there was no malice in her heart. She was impulsive and made no attempt to conceal her feeling; indeed, that would have been impossible, for her face was an index to every passing emotion.

"Mary found much difficulty in getting along smoothly with an Episcopal student of theology, who was a tutor in the Todd family. With all of Mary's efforts to be agreeable, there was nothing but discord between them. Having an ill-grounded and unjust suspicion that she was on all occasions laughing at him, or trying to insult him, he waged a war without cause."

Mr. Todd was frequently absent on business, and Mrs. Todd by reason of illness unable to come to the dining room. "One morning on such an occasion [writes Elizabeth] Mary and I went to the breakfast room. Mary took her seat at the head of the table and Mr. ——, the young tutor, took the seat at the foot, I on the other side. Grace was said with due reverence and then we commenced with keen appetites on the feast of good things before us. We had some remarkably fine maple syrup. Mary helped me and offered some to Mr. —— with the remark that she understood the Yankees always ate molasses with everything. It was the word 'Yankee,' I suppose, that raised the storm. He was greatly irritated. With a black frown and rolling his R's more than usual, he spoke with great emphasis. 'Miss Mary,' he said, 'there is a point beyond endurance which I cannot and will not stand.'

"Mary was, you must remember, one of a large family of boys and girls who jested much and seized on the slightest pretext to tease each other unmercifully. The young tutor looked so fierce and his wrath so great to have been occasioned by such a small amount of teasing, and the scene was so ludicrous to Mary that she leaned back in her chair and laughed so merrily and

contagiously that even Mr. ——'s anger was dissipated
and he joined in our laughter. The laughter acted like
a charm and the rest of that day we three sailed on a
calm sea of good humor."

Mary was very fond of horseback riding. She and
her cousin Margaret Stuart often were seen cantering
through Lexington. It was before the day of cross-
saddles for women but they had perfect balance on
their sidesaddles. They wore plumes in their hats
sweeping to their shoulders and long skirts which
whipped in the wind with the quick stride of their fine-
bred, spirited Kentucky horses. Often there would be
quite a cavalcade of young people galloping out to
some party in the country.

CHAPTER IV

THE siren voice of Illinois had for years been enchanting Kentucky. There had been such an exodus to the Prairie State that by 1836 Illinois was two-thirds composed of Kentuckians. Mary Todd, now eighteen and just finished at Madame Mentelle's school, heard this siren call through an invitation to visit her two sisters, Mrs. Ninian Edwards and Mrs. William Wallace.

Mary, on this first visit to Springfield, found herself by no means a stranger in the midst of a delightful society of cultured, intellectual people, among the most prominent of whom were members of her own family. Here were many aspiring young men, politically ambitious. Everywhere there was a Western breeziness and stir—surroundings delightful to Mary, just arrived from a quiet, sleepy town jogging along in its sureness of fine schools, acres of magnificent cultivated blue-grass farms, handsome houses, a settled social life, contentment, peace, and plenty. No need for stir or excitement.

Mary, full of life and animation, was a great toast among her kinspeople who met her with open arms and vied with each other in entertaining her. All of them wanted to hear Lexington news told in Mary's own spicy fashion. She, fresh, young, and enthusiastic, was an ardent Whig like themselves, and could tell them the latest gossip of all the politicians in Kentucky. She gave her own views with vigor on the subject of slavery. She said that her stepmother agreed with her, indeed, that all the Humphreys believed, like Henry Clay, in the gradual emancipation of the slaves, and the preservation of the Union by compromises on its extension. She was interesting to old and young alike. To the older ones she showed a mature, cultivated mind, and among the younger and more frivolous ones her beautiful clothes and graceful dancing made her an object of interest and pride.

Not only Scotch but Southern, the Todds with the Stuarts and other connections by marriage, formed in Springfield a veritable clan in loyalty and mutual affection.

Dr. John Todd, a brother of Robert Smith Todd, was a practicing physician. His two daughters, Elizabeth and Fanny, were about Mary's age and became her life-long friends: Elizabeth Todd became the wife of Mr. Grimsley, and, after his death, of the Reverend John H. Brown; and Fanny married Thomas Shelby, grandson of Isaac Shelby, first governor of Kentucky.

John Todd Stuart, her first cousin, lived in Spring-field with his family of six children. He had moved there after his admission to the bar at the age of twenty-one, and at once became prominent in his profession. He was the recognized leader of the Whig party in his adopted State, serving three terms in Congress,—the first two terms as a Whig, the last term in 1862 as a Democrat.

It was John Todd Stuart who persuaded Lincoln to study law. Judge David Davis, of the United States Supreme Court, in an address on Abraham Lincoln before the Illinois Bar Association, says:

"The part which Stuart took in shaping Lincoln's destiny is not generally known outside the circle of their immediate friends. They lodged at the same house and occupied the same bed during the session of the Legislature (at Vandalia). Both were Whigs in politics and trusted friends, and each esteemed aright the abilities of the other. Both were honest men, with deep convictions, and were appreciated by their fellow members. The one was liberally educated and a lawyer, the other uneducated and engaged in the humble occupation of land surveyor.

"Stuart saw at once that there must be a change of occupation to give Lincoln a fair start in life, and that the study and practice of law were necessary to stimulate his ambition and develop his faculties. When the subject was introduced it appeared that Lincoln had never entertained the idea of becoming a lawyer, and stated difficulties which he deemed insurmountable. These Stuart overcame, and Lincoln agreed to give the matter thoughtful consideration. The result was that he yielded to Stuart's solicitations, and read law at his country home, some distance from Springfield, under the direction of Stuart, and with books loaned by him for the purpose. On Lincoln's admission to the bar Stuart formed a partnership with him, which continued, I think, until Stuart went to Congress.

"Every lawyer and every thoughtful and intelligent person can readily see the influence which the choice of the legal profession had on Lincoln's life."

Lincoln had served in the Black Hawk War with Major John T. Stuart, and there they had formed the tie made by fellow soldiers who had been companions through suspense, hardship, and danger. Many men who later entered prominently into Lincoln's life were in the Black Hawk War, with him. There were Jefferson Davis, a Kentuckian by birth who was to be President of the Southern Confederacy; General Robert Anderson, later commander of the Federal garrison fired upon at Fort Sumter; Colonel Zachary Taylor;

General Winfield Scott, and Lieutenant Albert Sidney Johnston, afterwards a Confederate general.

Stuart, just before Mary came to Springfield, had formed a law partnership with Lincoln. Mary, who was hearing many stories of the new law partner, felt that if "Cousin John," a man whom she admired next to her father and Henry Clay, had selected this close associate he must be the same order of man as her cousin.

But the stories from various sources were so conflicting. He was uncouth—and moody; he was sad—and could make men weep. Groups of his cronies were convulsed with laughter at his irresistibly funny and pat anecdotes—he was shy and sometimes dull in society. Large audiences were thrilled by his statesmanlike eloquence—he was only a log-rolling politician. He was clean shaven and his linen was immaculate—he often wore jeans and was careless of his personal appearance.

These were the opinions Mary heard from her older friends and relatives. The young people declared that while Lincoln cared less for sociey than for law and politics, he was as well dressed as any other man, wearing satin vest, stock, and broadcloth to parties and cotillions, entering into social life with good-natured enthusiasm, although he cared little for dancing. Some of the girls pronounced him awkward and shy, others said he was homely but perfectly at ease. The young men reported that at times he avoided company and went off into the country by himself, notably at the time of his admission to the bar, a time when a successful aspirant is wont to keep himself in evidence. They said that he was the center of every gathering of men interested in politics; that while he sought the company of older men, he and a few of his associates were forming a lyceum of young men to discuss the political problems of the day.

What was Mary to think?

It was Mr. Stuart who gave her an insight into Lincoln's real character. She heard him tell, at a family gathering, of Lincoln's amusing blunders in the Black Hawk War; of how, when he could not remember the word of command "to get his company endwise," he loudly shouted: "This company is dismissed for two minutes, when it will fall in again on the other side of the gate."

He told, too, how Lincoln suffered a disgrace on account of the lawlessness of the privates of his company who unknown to him, their captain, had stolen a quantity of whisky and were too drunk to fall in when the order was given to march. For this misdemeanor they were punished vicariously by Lincoln's superior officer ordering him to wear a wooden sword for two days, much to his embarrassment. Mary laughed delightedly at the anecdote, but with a slight gesture of contempt for the ignorant young backwoodsman.

Noting her feelings, Stuart launched into a panegyric of Lincoln's intellect. Mary idolized intellect. He told her how quickly Lincoln had mastered the science of law; how keen and honest his insight into matters of right and wrong; how unerring his judgment; how quick-witted he proved himself in quoting sentences applicable to a particular case from the Bible, Shakespeare, Robert Burns, or other authors he had absorbed and made his own; how surprisingly he had mastered the English language and how clearly, forcibly and eloquently he expressed his thought. Then with a note of tenderness Stuart described the dignity and nobility of his partner in defending the just cause of a poor and ignorant man. He told of his scorn for an ignoble action and of his scathing ridicule of a political demagogue in the opposition, making the audience roar with laughter and converting their sympathies and votes to his own side.

Mary's brothers-in-law, William Wallace and Ninian Edwards, also had many stories to tell. Her "Cousin Steve" (Stephen T. Logan), in talking to her of Lincoln, declared he had the physical strength of a giant. Once, when a fight broke out in Lincoln's audience and one of his supporters was being worsted, he stepped down from the platform and threw the quarrelsome "enemy" some ten or twelve feet, then nonchalantly stepped back on the platform and resumed his speech as if nothing had happened. He told her that during the session of the Ninth Assembly, in Vandalia, and at the extra session called in December, 1835, when he and Lincoln were fellow legislators, his acquaintance with Lincoln had crystallized into a firm friendship. He had found Lincoln modest, unaffected and simple in manner, and honest, candid, and shrewd in politics.

"Last summer," he continued, "to illustrate Lincoln's shrewdness, he had to answer a personal attack when electioneering. One of his rival candidates stated publicly that if facts in his possession were known to the public Lincoln would lose his chance of success at the polls. Lincoln answered his mysterious accuser thus: "No one [he wrote his rival] has needed favors more than I, and generally few have been less unwilling to accept them; but in this case favor to me would be injustice to the public and therefore I must beg your pardon for declining it. That I once had the confidence of the people of Sangamon County is sufficiently evident; and if I have done anything, either by design or misadventure, which if known would subject me to a forfeiture of that confidence, he that knows of that thing and conceals it is a traitor to his country's interest.

"I find myself wholly unable to form any conjecture of what fact or facts, real or supposed, you spoke, but my opinion of your veracity will not permit me for a moment to doubt that you at least believed what you said. I am flattered with the personal regard you manifested for me; but I do hope that on mature reflection you will view the public interest as a paramount consideration and therefore let the worst come."

Even her "Cousin Stephen" was satisfied at Mary's appreciation of the crushing candor in this note; but she wanted to meet this man and judge for herself. An uneducated backwoodsman had won the golden opinion of her able and cultured relatives and friends, what a phenomenon! But where was this man most of all spoken of, where was Abraham Lincoln, whose name and stories were eternally on the lips of all the people of Springfield?

Mary's curiosity grew keener each day, but its gratification was doomed to disappointment. That she did not meet Abraham Lincoln during this three months' visit is not surprising. He must have had little time for society. He had just formed his first law partnership. He was a member of the Tenth Assembly and they were feverishly planning internal improvements which they hoped would place Illinois on a par with New York—railroads, canals, river improvements, bridges —planning ways and means to finance all these schemes. The Whigs had won a victory over the Democrats in having the capitol moved from Vandalia to Springfield. The Democrats claimed trickery and chicanery, so an extra session was called in the summer at Vandalia, and Lincoln had a bitter fight with L. D. Ewing who wanted to keep the capitol at Vandalia. All this Mary heard with keen interest and excitement.

Mary met at this time another one of Lincoln's intimate associates and friends, John J. Hardin, a Kentuckian who had adopted Illinois and had many stories to tell Mary of the young politician.

Mary recalled to Hardin's mind a letter he had written in 1830 to her relative, Robert W. Scott, of Frankfort, Kentucky. This letter which was of much interest to the Todds was sent to one and then another of the family, and Mary, who was twelve years old at the time, remembered hearing her father read it aloud to her stepmother.

The letter was written from Jacksonville, September 24, 1830.

"Dear Scott:

"Our country at present is swarming with travellers. It appears as if the flood gates of Kentucky had broken loose, and her population set free had naturally turned their course to Illinois and Missouri. From the numbers already arrived, and the reports they bring, added to the knowledge we have of those on the road, it seems probable that the immigration will be greater this fall. Jacksonville is on the most direct route from Louisville to Palmyra, Mo., we therefore see a great number who are on the road to that place. In nine cases out of ten they remark that if they could bring their negroes here they would go no further. There are a great many instances of persons who after travelling through Mo. and then coming here on their return resolved not to go to Mo., nor will they come here, as this is a free State. By which means you retain many of your Kentucky population. The great objection to travellers to this country is the scarcity of timber. Being accustomed to land all covered over with timber they view a prairie as a barren waste. Since my first residence here my opinions have undergone considerable change. Then I looked at this country much as they do now, but from my knowledge of facts and the experience of older men the conclusion come to is, that there is timber enough. . . .

"Our society is composed of every nation, tribe and kindred. We have a considerable English Colony settled in one of the finest parts of the country, ten or twelve families arrived this summer direct from England and who started for this place. These with those we had before will make 40 or 50 families The population of the county is about two-thirds Kentuckian, many of them men of standing and wealth in Kentucky. The offices however are

"ELLERSLY"

This house, situated on a large farm, was built about 1785 by General Levi Todd (Mary Todd Lincoln's grandfather). The place he named Ellersly in honor of a small village, the home of the Todds in Scotland. Robert Smith Todd was born in this house February 25, 1791. The place now belongs to the Lexington Water Company

MARY TODD'S BIRTHPLACE

The home of Robert Smith Todd on Short Street, Lexington, Kentucky. Mary was born here December 13, 1818. This photograph was made after a fire had destroyed all but the outside walls

nearly all held by Eastern people. This is the reason given.
Edwards when sent here as territorial governor, supposing
it was a free state it would be settled by western people,
to keep them in favor appointed eastern men for judges etc.,
these appointed their clerks of the same stamp. . . . In
Jacksonville we have some very intelligent and decent
Yankees who are an addition to our society or rather they
form a society for themselves, for in truth there is no great
social intercourse between them and the Kentuckians. It is
surprising however how fast we are improving our society
by well informed Kentuckians settling amongst us. Many
families have come in since I did. General Duncan our
member to Congress has purchased him a farm on the edge
of town and has moved to it.

"Concerning the great and important matter of girls, it
is not in my power to boast much. We have some sprightly
ladies in town though they are few and indeed when this
state is compared to yours in that respect it falls short
indeed. I think it would improve if it were not for one
reason, the girls get married so soon there is no time for
improvement. Enterprising young men are numerous and
when they have entered their land they want wives, and
will have them. It has occurred to me that a considerable
speculation might be made by a qualified person who would
bring out a cargo of the ladies. You recollect in the first
settlement of Virginia a cargo of that description was
brought in and sold for 150 pounds of tobacco per head.
If they should be landed here shortly they might command
in market at least several head of cattle apiece. Besides it

would be a very great accommodation to many young ladies of my acquaintance who have been a long time trying to make an equal swap but as yet have not succeeded. Please give this matter an attentive consideration.

"The important question whether I would advise other young men to come here, must now be considered. There are a certain description of young men who ought never to leave their mothers' apron strings and who know not how to conduct themselves when abroad but whine and talk about home as tho' there was no other place decent people could live. These have no business here. Another class with talent and no energy in a short time become dissatisfied—they need the fostering hand of encouragement and flattery and for such there is no place here. . . . There is still another class, my friend, who are willing to take things as they find them, to think of home as a hallowed spot yet not contrast it with a county six years old and not yet populated. . . . If there are any such as these in your knowledge give them all encouragement to come here. My love to the girls and tell them, bless their hearts, I should like to see a cargo shortly. . . .

Your friend,
John J. Hardin."

Mary laughingly quoted the last sentence in Hardin's letter which she had remembered for six years. "Well, little cousin," said Hardin, "while you are one of a belated cargo, you are not too late to help some poor fellow fight the battle of life."

CHAPTER V

A KENTUCKY GIANT

UPON Mary's return home from the Illinois capital her father expressed a wish that she should accept an invitation to visit his brother's family in Columbia, Missouri. But Mary, again at home, was having too good a time to wish to leave at once. She must see all her friends first, she must cuddle all her little sisters, and brothers. Then, a round of family dinners and parties behind her, Mary with a rejuvenated wardrobe started on her journey, not to Missouri, but to Illinois, for her sisters had been besieging her with letters to come back to Springfield for a longer visit and Mary, nothing loath, had begged to be allowed to do so. At first she met with a refusal from her parents, but Mary came of pioneer people who would have been swallowed up in the wilderness if they had not been dominant, willful, and determined and these traits, which she fully inherited, finally gained her point.

There was no quarrel with her stepmother as certain biographers state; but truth to tell, the stir and excitement of the young capital had fired Mary's imagination. So, gaining the consent of her parents in 1839, she went to Springfield on a prolonged visit to her sister, Mrs. Ninian Edwards. There, soon after her arrival, Mary, under the wing of Mrs. Edwards, made her first appearance at a cotillion. The scene was brilliant enough to have pleased Mary had she been only an onlooker. The girls in their flowerlike frocks, the soft bursts of laughter, the many gleaming candles casting long wavering lines of light across the polished floor, the cadenced strains of a waltz making dreamy accompaniment to the gliding feet of the dancers. The beaux who remembered Mary flocked around her, importuning her for the first dance. As she slowly circled the room her attention was attracted by the appearance of a tall, spare, but powerfully built man, in earnest conversation with her brother-in-law. His face was a fascinating combination of poetic mysticism, earnest purpose, and quaint humor. Just the kind of strength and ruggedness, too, that had attracted Mary when as a little girl she had declared "Henry Clay is the handsomest man in town."

"Who is that man?" she asked with some excitement in her voice, losing for the moment her little Southern drawl. She had already divined that he must be the much talked of Lincoln.

Their eyes met. His with a searching, appraising glance. Shyly Mary glanced at him through half-closed eyes. Her heart beat a little faster and the faint wild rose in her cheeks deepened.

Mary, although not strictly beautiful, was more than pretty. She had a broad white forehead, eyebrows sharply but delicately marked, a straight nose, short upper lip and an expressive mouth curling into an adorable slow coming smile that brought dimples into her cheeks and glinted in her long-lashed, blue eyes. Those eyes, shaded by their long, silky fringe, gave an impression of dewy violet shyness contradicted fascinatingly by the spirited carriage of her head. She was vital, brilliant, witty, and well trained in all the social graces from earliest childhood. She could now, without rebuke, wear the coveted hoop skirts of her childish desire, and with skirts frosted with lace and ruffles she ballooned and curtsied in the lovely embroidered French swisses and muslins brought up to her from New Orleans by her father.

In stockings and slippers to match the color of her gown, all pink and white, she danced and swayed as lightly and gayly as a branch of fragrant apple blossoms in a gentle spring breeze. From her pink dimpled cheeks to her sophisticated pink satin slippers, she was a fascinating, alluring creature, and Abraham Lincoln in his black satin waistcoat and high black satin stock was himself no mean figure of fashion. As a young man he looked the poet that he really was at heart.

His gray eyes lighted with interest as he watched Mary's animated, piquant face and caught little snatching glimpses of satin slipper straps and gleaming silk-clad ankles under billowing masses of lace and organdy, as her hoops swayed in rhythm to the waltz music. Although he cared little for dancing, preferring to look on or talk to some of the more agreeable older members of an assemblage, he could not resist this bewitching creature and on being presented to her, he said:

"Miss Todd, I want to dance with you the worst way."

And Mary, with a roguish smile and a twinkle in her eyes, said after the party in recounting the incident to her cousin Elizabeth Todd, "And he certainly did."

Though Mary did not dance again that evening with Mr. Lincoln she felt his eyes were following her and when during an intermission she saw him making a bee line in her direction, she promptly, too promptly, held her program out that he might see for himself that it was filled to overflowing. She did not wish again to put in jeopardy her little pink satin slippers. But the dimple in her cheek seemed to say, "I am sorry."

Mr. Lincoln made an appointment to call the following evening, a scintillating exchange of wit and humor passing between them. It pleased him that she understood and discussed politics with subtle discernment. From that time they were on all occasions drawn irresistibly together. They discovered new bonds in common.

Now that Mary could form her own judgment of Lincoln, she hardly knew what to think. He was in appearance a dreamer, yet from his records, practical, and ready to take advantage of every opportunity to improve himself. He was certainly not the ill-dressed man some people said he was (Mary attached importance to dress), but was as conventionally clad as all the other young men she met. She might have known, of course, that her cousin John Stuart would hardly have taken into his office for a partner a man whose appearance or manner could cast a reflection on a dignified firm. Also, of course, when Lincoln was traveling through the country electioneering he was shrewd enough to know, having been a backwoodsman himself, that broadcloth, even if frayed and dusty, would not win as many votes among the farmers as jeans.

Mary heard on all sides that Lincoln was the life of a party of men and that one anecdote after another rolled readily off his tongue, but that his tongue was

tied in the presence of ladies. She found this as much
a fable as the story that he appeared in jeans when
broadcloth would be a more appropriate garb. If now
and then he called when in a quiet thoughtful mood,
that mattered not at all to Mary who was an enthusiastic talker and enjoyed an appreciative audience. And
when Lincoln did break his silence, he was keen and
expressed some thought in forceful fashion starting
Mary off again. They often read aloud to each other
and criticized some book or poem. The institution of
slavery they both condemned, hoping that it would not
be extended beyond its present boundaries.

Altogether, Mary found in Lincoln the most congenial mind she had ever met. One evening lingering
over coffee and cake in the dining room, Mary and her
sister were recalling with much amusement the super-
stitions of their childhood, when they heard Mr. Lincoln's voice in the hall.

"Bring Mr. Lincoln in here," Mrs. Edwards directed the servant. Greetings exchanged, she motioned
him to a chair beside herself and helping him to some
cake, said, glancing at Mary, "This cake is not as light
as usual. You see, I made it on Friday—that is the
reason it is sad, I suppose. Never," she said with mock
seriousness, "commence anything on that unlucky day."
"Oh," said Mary laughing, "I would not think of

doing such a thing! I cut out an organdy frock on Friday, two years ago, and it is still unfinished. Since then, I always propitiate the Fates, the Furies, and the Fairies. You see," she said, turning to Mr. Lincoln, "my sister and I are part Scotch and we believe in fairies. I have hunted for the magic circle where they dance, and I am sure I have heard the faint elusive music of fairy bells."

"And the elfin horns faintly blowing?" asked Mr. Lincoln, entering into her poetic mood. "I believe in fairies myself," he added, looking at her admiringly. "I am sure that one of them must have been your godmother. She fell in love with you in your cradle and showered you with all her choicest gifts. You and your sister must have been prime favorites of that generous lady," he said, bowing courteously to Mrs. Edwards.

"You shall have a glass of sherry for that pretty compliment," exclaimed Mrs. Edwards who had filled him a wine glass. As Mr. Lincoln smilingly shook his head, she said, "I am sorry I have no hard cider to offer you; you are such a staunch Whig you would not refuse to drink a toast with us to William Henry Harrison in the beverage so acclaimed in his log-cabin and hard-cider canvass. "No," said Mr. Lincoln, with a laugh, "for I was brought up in a log cabin and raised on hard cider." "As were all our sturdy pioneers in Kentucky," said Mrs. Edwards. "Many distinguished men commenced life in the early days in a log fort or a cozy, chinked cabin with a generous big chimney, typical of their big generous hearts. By the way, Mary has just accepted an invitation to visit the family of our uncle, Judge David Todd in Missouri, who is as ardent a Whig as you. They have promised her a most interesting and exciting time, since all the politicians in that State will be assembled at Rocheport only a short distance from uncle's home in Columbia." Mary and Mr. Lincoln exchanged a quiet glance. He had heard of this contemplated visit and together they had conceived a romantic plan to meet each other during this political rally.

Mary had never met her father's three brothers, who had left Kentucky and had settled in Missouri in 1817. Sam Todd was the uncle who had been captured by the Indians and adopted by an old squaw. Masquerading as her son, he had been considered a member of the tribe for three years, until he managed to escape. Mary never tired of hearing this thrilling story over and over again. Whigs like all the Todds, David had been elected circuit judge, and Roger North, circuit clerk. They were all solid, substantial citizens.

Judge Todd, accompanied by Mary and his daughter Ann, went to Rocheport. There were four steamboat loads of cheering enthusiastic Whigs steaming up the Missouri River with bands of music playing and flags and Harrison banners flying. The boat on which Mr. Lincoln had taken passage went aground on a sand bar and the disappointed passengers failed to reach the big political rally. Mr. Lincoln did not fail, however, to reach Columbia, and the next Sunday he and Mary were occupying the Todd pew in the Presbyterian Church.

Mary and her cousin Ann E. Todd became great friends. Among the young men paying homage to the two girls was a wealthy young Missourian named Campbell, and when Ann later visited Mrs. Edwards in Springfield the attentions of Joshua Speed and numerous other beaux counted as nothing beside the love letters that daily arrived from the devoted Mr. Campbell.[1] Ann married him soon after she returned to Columbia, and they lived in Boonville, Missouri. One son, Quint Campbell, was a newspaper writer.

When Mary returned to Springfield, she kept her uncle Dr. John Todd chuckling over the anecdotes she

[1] Dr. William E. Barton, in *The Women Lincoln Loved*, having in mind, no doubt, a letter written by Lincoln, May 18, 1843, to his friend Joshua Speed, in which Lincoln mentions the fact: "Ann Todd was married something more than a year since to a fellow by the name of Campbell * * *," jumped to a false conclusion when he stated that Ann Todd (Mary's sister) was married twice, first to a Mr. Campbell and then to Mr. C. M. Smith. The Ann Todd alluded to in Mr. Lincoln's letter was Ann E. Todd, the daughter of Judge David Todd of Columbia, Missouri.

had heard of his brother David. "Every day after dinner," she related, "and before returning to the court-
house, it was uncle's custom to take a short nap. On
account of company for dinner one day he was deprived
of his forty winks. One of the lawyers was making a
long argument to the jury and Uncle David went to
sleep on the bench. He awoke in a moment and inter-
rupting the lawyer in his argument, said, "Mr. Clerk,
enter up a fine of ten dollars against David Todd for
contempt of court. I'll break up this habit of going to
sleep in daylight or I'll break the court." "Yes," said
her Uncle John, "that is like David, he is the soul of
honesty, though he is somewhat of a spendthrift."

The meeting of Mary and Mr. Lincoln in Missouri
brought their incipient love affair closer to a definite
understanding.

That Lincoln did not observe the conventionalities of
society alternately amused and irritated Mary although
she realized that many things he did not know or do
must be ingrained and carefully taught in childhood,
by precept and example, and that if merely conformed
to later in life is only an artificial veneer more easily
peeled off than put on. When Mary slyly poked fun
at him for committing some faux pas he would look at
her quizzically, his gray eyes twinkling, as if to say,
"How can you attach such great importance to matters

so trivial?" and Mary's color would deepen as though caught in a petty meanness, or if she spoke sharply in reproof, the hurt look in his eyes made her repentant and almost ready to weep. "Mary could make a bishop forget his prayers," chuckled Ninian Edwards one day when Mary mimicked the mannerisms of some of her beaux with unflattering fidelity, although her imitation of Lincoln was never so full of spice.

"I hear the Yankee, the Irishman and our rough diamond from Kentucky were here last night," joked her cousin Stephen Logan. "How many more have you on the string, Mary?" "Are they not enough?" she replied. "Which of them do you fear the most?" "I fear I am in grave danger," said Logan, "of having to welcome a Yankee cousin." "Never!" said Mary. "The Yankee, as you call Mr. Douglas, differs from me too widely in politics. We would quarrel about Henry Clay. And Jimmy Sheilds, the Irishman, has too lately kissed the Blarney Stone for me to believe he really means half of his compliments, and the rough diamond ——" "The rough diamond," interrupted Cousin Steve, "is much too rugged for your little white hands to attempt to polish." "To polish a stone like that," said Mary dreamily, "would be the task of a lifetime, but what a joy to see the beauty and brilliance shine out more clearly each day! The important thing

is the diamond itself, clear and flawless under its film."
"Whew!" whistled the astonished Cousin Steve, "you
don't mean you would seriously consider it?" "Why
not?" quickly countered Mary with some heat. "He
is one of your best friends. You have told me time
and again you never met a man with more ability, more
native intellect." "But," quietly interposed Mrs. Edwards, "Mary is not thinking of Mr. Lincoln in the
light of a lover, Cousin Steve, he is merely one of her
most agreeable friends and not one whit more agreeable
than Mr. Douglas or several others."

Still, her cousins from this time on noticed that Mary
flared into defense at the least criticism of Lincoln,
although she herself still made a little—a very little—
mild fun of the young lawyer. Mr. and Mrs. Edwards
at last became alarmed at Mary's evident preference,
and feeling their responsibility as her guardians, they
strongly objected and pointed out to Mary the incon-
gruity of such a marriage. Although Mr. Lincoln was
honorable, able, and popular, his future, they said, was
nebulous, his family relations were on a different social
plane. His education had been desultory. He had no
culture, he was ignorant of social forms and customs, he
was indifferent to social position.

Why couldn't she fancy some man possessing these
qualities which Lincoln lacked? Why not fancy

Stephen A. Douglas or some other of the promising young men in love with her? Douglas, they reminded her, although he had no bank account, was an educated and polished young man, a rising young politician with a bright future that should more than satisfy the most ambitious woman. Four years younger than Lincoln, he had already achieved higher political honors and already was mentioned for Congress. He might become senator; perhaps, even President. From every point of view nothing could be more desirable than a marriage with him.

Mary listened with an impassive face. She knew all this. She had told herself over and over again that Douglas from a socially ambitious point of view would be a more desirable husband, but something deep down in the sad gray eyes of Lincoln drew her very heart out of her breast with longing and tenderness. She was drawn as naturally and irresistibly to Lincoln as if through some law of spiritual gravitation. Not that she sometimes did not have a bitter struggle with herself. When Lincoln would carelessly ignore some social custom or forget an engagement, she would then resentfully wish she could decide in favor of Douglas. Mary had been as fascinated with Mr. Lincoln's personality from their very first meeting as he had been with her grace and wit. Each found in the other the novelty which is most winsome to lovers. He found in her a bubbling fun, an enthusiastic love of life. She in turn was intrigued by his moodiness, his sincerity and honesty, his freedom from the pretty flatteries and the conventional gallantries of the men in her social set. He had never met a woman like Mary Todd, suave, equal to any social emergency. She had found for the first time a young man with a mentality dominating yet in accord with her own.

When Mary's sister, Mrs. Edwards, confided to her sisters and other relatives in Springfield her fear that Mary was about to make a serious matrimonial mistake, they were amused, believing this to be only one more of Mary's flirtations, for she was an incorrigible flirt. But when they realized she was in earnest they showered her with advice and objections. Her sisters plainly gave her that "piece of mind" which "never impoverishes the giver nor enriches the receiver." Altogether, Mary was not having a peaceful time. Neither, for that matter, was Lincoln, for gossip was drifting to his ears that he was not considered a desirable addition to the family by Mary's relatives.

The handsome home of the Edwards' now became the center of a social whirl of gayety. They entertained with lavish Southern hospitality, and the house was thronged with laughing young girls and eligible young men. But Mary was not to be diverted from her choice.

Being socially prominent, she was frequently quoted: "Mary Todd said" thus and so, or "Mary Todd did this or that," construed variously as the narrators or auditors were friendly or otherwise. She was sharply criticized for her drive on a dray. She had gone on foot to call on some friends within walking distance of the Edwards home. A heavy shower having fallen during her call, she was dismayed on starting home to see the deep black mud of the streets. She glanced ruefully down at her thin modish gray gaiters and snowy white, belaced petticoats, but her nimble wit and independent spirit were equal to the emergency. With her whimsical smile she summoned a passing dray to take her home. Waving gayly and victoriously to the acquaintances she passed on the way, she jolted home with dry gaiters and dainty petticoats. Only one who has seen the deep, rich, black soil of Illinois on a rainy day can fully appreciate the wisdom of this unusual and apparently eccentric drive.

Lincoln heard Mary quoted almost as often as she delightedly listened to anecdotes of him, and so these two people, trained so differently, found each other.

Mary had always lived in an atmosphere of thought and books, of ambition to attain the best in the mental, spiritual, and material world, on a social plane where the refinements and amenities of life were considered important and occupied a large share of time and attention. Thanks to the strong arms and active brains of her Indian-fighting ancestors, her place in the sun had been won and puncheon floors had long since been replaced by floors waxed and polished like mirrors.

Lincoln's people, on the other hand, had not yet struggled up from the dirt and puncheon floors. In pioneer days they had unfortunately located in Kentucky on poor, rocky soil that no amount of toil would bring to produce abundantly. No wonder the family grew apathetic and discouraged. What was the use! Abraham Lincoln knew from personal experience, toil, suffering, deprivation, and discouragement, but being a dreamer and a poet by nature and having the "divine urge" of a rich, strong, and many-sided mentality, he was spurred on and on.

While Mary's engagement to Mr. Lincoln had not been formally announced, her family and friends knew that she and Lincoln had reached an understanding. Like most engaged lovers, they had their heated disputes, jealousies, lovers' quarrels, swift reconciliations, and intervals of loving understanding. When Lincoln, ten years older than Mary and schooled by bitter experience, realized that he was about to assume the responsibility for the support and happiness of a young women unused to deprivations of any kind, he became panic-stricken. A few years before he had written a former sweetheart, Mary Owens, that he feared he could not make her happy on account of the "flourishing around in carriages" of the Springfield wealthy class. And now—he was engaged to sparkling, happy, high-spirited Mary Todd, a petted, fêted society girl, a little spoiled by all the adulation and attention she was constantly receiving. How could he supply all her demands? How give her lovely clothes, pin money, a carriage; indeed, to face the facts, how could he provide her with what she would deem the very essentials of life? Would her love turn to humiliation and harden into indifference were she deprived of the luxuries to which she had been accustomed? He had been deeply hurt by the opposition of Mary's family. Those who knew her most intimately thought she would be unhappy with a poor man. Were they right? In the candor of self-examination, did he think himself, struggling for a foothold in his profession, unlearned in social graces, a suitable husband for Mary? Suppose she regretted too late that she had not made the brilliant marriage her family had a right to expect. That they loved each other was not now the case in point. His pride and love were in mortal combat. Between

these conflicting emotions he became obsessed by the
deep melancholy latent in his being. Perhaps he and
Mary had made a mistake in selecting each other, he
mused moodily, with his chin sunk in his hands.

With a sigh he came out of these unhappy reflections
to remember with a start that the hour of his engagement to take Mary to a party had passed. When he
reached the Edwards home, breathless from his hurried
walk and disturbed in mind, he found Mary had gone.
Following quickly, he discovered her dancing happily
with Stephen Douglas, ever ready to seize upon opportunities and never forgetful of social engagements.

Mary noticed Lincoln's arrival, though apparently
she did not vouchsafe so much as a glance in her tardy
lover's direction, but flirted ostentatiously with the delighted Douglas. Seeing this, Lincoln let the apology
which he was about to make die on his lips and, a
twinge of jealousy contracting his heart, he turned
abruptly and left the house. "Well, so be it, she has
made her own choice," he felt. Perhaps it is better so.
He could neither think clearly, work nor sleep; the
situation was unbearable. He determined to have a
talk with Mary and end it all.

On New Year's day there was the usual big family
gathering at the Edwards home; dinner had been joyous and prolonged, lasting from four until seven

o'clock. The guests had departed, and Mary was alone. Seated before a glowing fire she was expecting her—lover, but she was totally unprepared for the effect her flirtation with Stephen Douglas had had on him. Lincoln appeared grim and determined. Without preamble he told her plainly that he intended to release her from her engagement. Mary was furiously angry; the pink in her cheeks glowed a deeper rose, and her eyes were a deeper blue as she told him in a strained, low voice that while she had loved him with her whole heart she now hoped and prayed never to see his detestable face again.

"Go," she cried with a stamp of her little foot, "and never, never, never come back."

Lincoln turned sadly and unsteadily away. And now that he had settled this love affair, in effect if not in manner, as he had planned—was he happy? Would she be happy? He knew now beyond a doubt, with a curious sinking of his heart, that Mary Todd had loved him, yes, still loved him. Had he made a terrible mistake and shattered the world for both of them? He wrote to John T. Stuart three weeks after the breaking of his engagement of the "deplorable state" of his mind, and added:

"I am now the most miserable man living. If what I

feel were equally distributed to the whole human family, there would not be one cheerful face on the earth."

The breaking of their engagement was known to all their friends. And while Lincoln was too wretched to keep his own council and wrote and talked of his unhappiness, Mary was too proud to show the hurt in her heart. Her family received the news with unalloyed joy and hoped that Mary's heart might be caught on the rebound by some more eligible man.

It seems hardly worth while for a member of Mary Todd's family to deny again that a wedding between Mary and Mr. Lincoln was arranged for the first of January, 1841, but Emilie Todd (Mrs. Ben Hardin Helm), Mary Todd's sister, who at this writing is living and possessed of all her faculties, declares Herndon's story to be absolutely false and a cruel reflection on the character of a noble man who would have been incapable of such an act of cruel cowardice as nonappearance at his own wedding. The preceding account of what happened on that "fatal" first of January, 1841, Mrs. Edwards told Mrs. Helm she had gathered brokenly from their sister Mary when Mary with tears in her eyes and a forced light laugh told her sister of her broken engagement.

Meanwhile Mr. Lincoln was ill. And hoping to find comfort and consolation in intimate talks, he visited

his friend Joshua F. Speed (on a farm near Louisville), who afterwards gave for publication letters
written to him in strictest confidence by Lincoln.   In
one of the letters Lincoln begs Speed not to show
the letters to anyone not even to his wife Fanny, unless
all the circumstances had already been told her.   In
spite of this entreaty, the letters were published for all
the world to see the heart laid bare for Speed's eyes
alone; though Mr. Speed, with "rare delicacy of feeling," states one biographer, "carefully stipulated that
the name of a certain lady be withheld from publication."   Pity that this rare delicacy of feeling had not
also been extended toward his confiding and trusting
friend!

But Mary did not droop, though her world seemed
dull indeed without her "Robin Adair."   She took her
amusements with spirit and gayety.   She did not wear
her heart on her sleeve.   Apparently she did not pine
for her lost lover, and Lincoln need not have been so
grieved over her unhappiness that he needs must write
of it to Speed.   He seems to have been greatly surprised
that Mary was enjoying herself so exceedingly, and exclaimed, "God be praised for that."   Subconsciously
though, he seems to have been chagrined that Mary apparently missed him so little that she could actually

enjoy herself without him, laughing and chatting with other friends as if no Lincoln existed.

Mr. Lincoln was now free from any entanglement with Mary Todd. His only source of unhappiness, he writes Speed, being one whom he had "contributed to make unhappy, I cannot but reproach myself for even wishing to be happy while she is otherwise." But this cause for his unhappiness did not exist. He thanked God that Mary was happy; and strange as it seemed to him, Mary *was* happy—the center of attraction at balls and parties, picnics and excursions.

He, lonely, puzzled, overwhelmed with melancholy, must have missed her bright repartee, the play of expression on her mobile face emphasizing the meaning of her words. Memories of their past love affair surely haunted him, and a longing grew in his heart for a sight of her mysterious little crooked smile curling into irregular dimples on each side of her mouth, a little deeper on her right cheek. He wished to hear again the soft Southern drawl in her cultured voice. The little drawl which quickened into an eager flow of words when she was interested or excited. An ardent wish for reconciliation must have filled his heart, for when Mrs. Simeon Francis by a friendly ruse brought the two together in her parlor and said, "Be friends again," there was no hesitation on the part of either as

Mary lifted her long lashes and met the love she expected to find in Lincoln's deep-set earnest gray eyes. They were one in mind and heart and as long as life lasted neither ever again doubted the other's faithful love.

From that time they had many quiet meetings in the home of Mrs. Francis, and Mrs. Edwards knew nothing of these meetings. Mary wanted no advice, no more criticism of the man she loved. Though he may not have always made flowery, flattering speeches, though he may have been at times almost too frank and candid, the warm admiration and love which glowed in his eyes fully satisfied her. Judging his heart by her own, she knew that he loved her, she had known it all along during the months of their estrangement; and she felt that his love would be strong and enduring, that the romance she had cherished from childhood's days would culminate in marriage to the hero of her fancy, and that they "would be happy ever after." Neither Mary nor Mr. Lincoln wanted the "pomp and circumstance" incident to a big wedding, such as the Edwards' had given her sister Frances when she was married to Dr. William Wallace, so they decided to have the marriage ceremony performed very quietly at the house of Mr. Dresser, the Episcopal minister in the presence of a few of their most intimate friends.

They both feared further opposition from Mary's family and were still resentful of past advice and criticism.

Mr. Lincoln meeting Mr. Edwards on the street, therefore, told him that he and Mary had decided to be married quietly at Mr. Dresser's house that evening.

Mr. Edwards, feeling responsible for Mary, exclaimed: "No, I am Mary's guardian and if she is married at all it must be from my house."

Mary was consulted, and after some discussion she and Mr. Lincoln agreed to Mr. Edwards' wishes. It was a bright cool morning in November and Mary fairly flew to the home of her uncle, Dr. John Todd, who was much beloved by his nieces, being so calm and quiet and affable. "Uncle," she cried excitedly, "you must go and tell my sister that Mr. Lincoln and I are to be married this evening," and turning to her cousin Elizabeth Todd, she asked her to put on her bonnet and go with her to make some purchases.

When they reached the Edwards home there was great excitement coupled with no little indignation, that such news should have been announced so suddenly that there was not time to make formal and suitable preparations for a wedding. But Dr. Todd was a suave and diplomatic advocate for Mary's cause and soon had them all in smiling good-humor. Mrs. Edwards said with a teasing laugh, "It is fortunate, Mary, that you selected this evening, for the Episcopal sewing society meets with me and my supper is already ordered." "But," said Mrs. Grimsley, Mary's cousin (Elizabeth Todd), in a statement to Miss Tarbell, "this comfortable little arrangement did not suit Mary," and Uncle John was sent post haste to inform Mr. Lincoln that the wedding would be deferred until the next evening.

The Episcopal minister, Mary's close relatives, and a few of the most intimate friends of the two were notified. It was a very small gathering, not more than thirty people. But in spite of such hurried preparations, one of the guests writes, "The entertainment was simple but in beautiful taste." The bride wore one of her lovely embroidered white muslin dresses. Miss Jayne, Miss Rodney, and Miss Elizabeth Todd were her bridesmaids.

The heavy black clouds that had been massing all day sent down great splashing tear drops; then with the rain beating down in roaring torrents, raging and rattling at doors and windows, Mary Todd became the wife of Abraham Lincoln.

This was on Friday, the fourth of November, 1842.

CHAPTER VI

PARTNERS

MR. AND MRS. LINCOLN commenced their married life at a little inn, "The Globe Tavern," primitive and devoid of anything like luxury. But for the modest sum of four dollars a week, it would have been surprising if the Widow Beck could have furnished her boarders more than the barest necessities of life.

Although such surroundings could not fail to be anything but distasteful to Mary, reared as she had been, she never murmured; nor did she utter a single complaint, even to any member of her own family. Indeed, they assert she seemed very happy. Mr. Lincoln also seemed satisfied and had lost some of the deep gloom which had affected him all his life, and for which historians have tried in vain to account.

Mary knew of this deep and settled melancholy in the nature of the man she married. She had been drawn to him in the first place by this dreamy pensiveness which appealed to the strain of romance and poetry in her nature. She had an irresistible impulse to impart cheer and gayety; to make smiles take the place of gloom in this man she so tenderly loved. That she might fill his life with the comforts and refinements he had always lacked would be her greatest joy; she felt she could be to him a real helpmate. He was careless about being warmly clad, and indifferent as to his meals; she intended to see that he should be more careful about his health, that when they went to housekeeping he should have nutritious, appetizing food, well served at a well-ordered, dainty table, there should be flowers and snowy damask. She looked forward with eagerness to the little home they would have together. Dreaming of this, she contentedly lived at the tavern, received her callers without complaint, and made no apology for her unlovely surroundings. Gay and happy, she went with Mr. Lincoln to concerts and to see any strolling players passing through Springfield. They went to see the elder Jefferson, the father of his more famous son Joe, who played in Springfield that winter. A circus, too, was great fun and not to be missed. Then the parties and the family dinners with her sisters and her Uncle John, and best of all, the quiet evenings together when they talked and made plans for the future. The year passed quickly.

Ever since his eldest daughter Elizabeth had married Ninian Edwards, Robert S. Todd had gone to Springfield always once, sometimes twice, a year to visit his daughters and his nephew John Todd Stuart. The arrival of Mary's first son, Robert Todd, born August 1, 1843, was the important occasion at one of these visits. "May God bless and protect my little namesake" he had prayed, and Mary had whispered a fervent "Amen."

From the Globe Tavern Mr. and Mrs. Lincoln went to housekeeping in a little cottage of their own on the corner of Eighth and Jackson Streets. The little home was painted white and had green shutters. It was sweet and fresh, and Mary loved it. She was exquisitely dainty, and her house was a reflection of herself, everything in good taste and in perfect order. She enjoyed her new responsibilities and to her spirited manner, which had attracted Lincoln in the first place, was now added a charming little air of dignity as befitted a householder, and the mother of a son.

As Mr. Lincoln's law practice increased and his finances improved, he and Mary added to this house a second story, and although Mary passionately loved beautiful and desirable things, because of the cost, she had to collect her furniture and rugs very slowly, and although she loved to make herself pretty and dainty for her husband, she did not burden him by incurring heavy debts. With discriminating taste she bought the materials, always of the best, and made her own dresses. Yet in spite of this small outlay, she gained the reputation of being extravagant. Many of her feminine critics on double the expense did not dress half so well.

In 1846 Mary Lincoln was the proud mother of another son, Edward Baker, born March 10. Eighteen months later her longing to have her Kentucky relatives see her two boys was to be gratified. She was homesick for a sight of the haunts of her childhood, for she had written: "Mother, dear, I have been dreaming of our sweet old garden. I want to see it again, and even if, at this time of the year, it should be under its blanket of snow, I could still, in my mind's eye, see Elizabeth strolling with me on the garden walk to the summer house."

So Mr. Lincoln, in 1847, now a member of Congress, took Mary home to visit her father in Lexington before settling his family for the winter in Washington. As it was Mary's first visit to Kentucky since her marriage, she anticipated with eagerness her home-coming. None of her younger brothers or sisters had ever seen her.

It was a cold day in November, and the wide hall was chilly as the door was thrown open to receive them. The whole family stood near the front door with welcoming arms and, in true patriarchal style, the colored contingent filled the rear of the hall to shake hands with the long absent one and "make a miration" over the babies. Mary came in first with little Eddie, the baby, in her arms.

"To my mind she was lovely," her sister Emilie says; "clear, sparkling, blue eyes, lovely smooth white skin with a fresh, faint wild-rose color in her cheeks; and glossy light brown hair, which fell in soft, short curls behind each ear. She was then about twenty-nine years of age.

"Mr. Lincoln followed her into the hall with his little son Robert Todd in his arms. He put the little fellow on the floor, and as he arose I remember thinking of Jack and the Beanstalk, and feared he might be the hungry giant of the story, he was so tall and looked so big with a long full black cloak over his shoulders and he wore a fur cap with ear straps which allowed but little of his face to be seen. Expecting to hear the 'Fee, fi, fo, fum!' I shrank closer to my mother and tried to hide behind her voluminous skirts. After shaking hands with all the grown-ups Mr. Lincoln turned and, lifting me in his arms, said, 'So this is little sister.' I was always after that called by him 'little sister.' His voice and smile banished my fear of the giant.

"Our brother Sam, who was attending college at Danville, Kentucky, came home to see sister Mary and his little nephews. He taught Robert to call him 'Uncle Sam' and, swelled with importance at the honor

of being an uncle, he swaggered around as proud as
Punch, much to the quiet amusement of the older ones
of the family. 'What a big handsome boy Sam has
grown to be,' said Sister Mary to mother, 'he was such
a little scrap of a baby.' 'Well,' said Sam laughing,
'I at least have had the grace to grow up and you are
still only a tiny little scrap hardly reaching to my shoulder. I hope my nephews will inherit their father's long
legs.' 'And their mother's lovely disposition' said
Mary making a little grimace at him.

"I do not recall how long the visit lasted, but I remember the romps with Bob, and that Mr. Lincoln was
so absorbed in books that our noisy play never seemed
to disturb him. His reading, they told me later, was
principally *Niles Register* and a book of miscellaneous
poems. The poem by Cowper on 'Slavery and the
Slave Trade,' he bracketed and even turned down the
page upon which it appeared. At this time he committed to memory 'Thanatopsis.' "

Mrs. Helm tells an amusing incident in connection
with this visit. Mrs. Todd's nephew, Joseph Humphreys, had traveled on the same train with the Lincolns without knowing who they were. Being alone,
with no impedimenta, he quickly covered the ground
between the railway station and the Todd home.
"Aunt Betsy," he exclaimed, "I was never so glad to

get off a train in my life. There were two lively youngsters on board who kept the whole train in a turmoil, and their long-legged father, instead of spanking the brats, looked pleased as Punch and aided and abetted the older one in mischief." Glancing out of the window at that moment he saw the "long-legged" man and the two "lively youngsters" in the Todd carriage, which had just stopped before the door. "Good Lord," he said in a panic, "there they are now." He promptly vanished and was not seen again during Mary's visit.

"Four years later," Mrs. Helm continues, "in the summer of 1851, Sister Mary returned to Kentucky; but our father had died in 1849 and her visit now was to my mother at her country place Buena Vista, about twenty miles west of Lexington on the Frankfort Pike. It was summertime and the house was filled with roses and other cut flowers in honor of our expected guest. She had with her, her two boys, Bob and Willie, little Eddie having died in February. I was now thirteen years old and could appreciate her winning personality. I hung around her fascinated, as she and my mother exchanged reminiscences, and gave each other family news. They talked of politics and the large issues of the day. Mary was a good and enthusiastic talker, very observant, seeing the ludicrous as well as the serious side of things. Her tears and laughter were very close together as she and my mother talked of the past.

"I remember how kind and courteous she was to the old slaves who, with many chuckles, reminded her of the pranks she used to play in her childhood. They were often the indignant victims. Old Chaney was grieved that 'Miss Mary didn't have no beaten biscuits at home because the po' white trash Irish didn't even know how to make good co'n bread.' And Mary, smiling but exasperated, with her notebook and pencil tried to take directions of, 'Jes a pinch—jes a leetle bit—sweetenin' to tas',' and so on. And Sally, our faithful old black mammy, usually so sweet tempered, was insufferably arrogant for days after Miss Mary wished she had just such a good old black nurse for little Willie.

"Robert, seven years old, played with our youngest brother Alec, a quick-tempered, red-headed, little rascal, who was so enchanted with his new sister that we were always trying to shoo him away for fear his clinging attentions and moist little kisses would annoy her; when she put one arm around Robert, the other arm must encircle Alec or there would be a wail of sorrow. The two little fellows scampered about on ponies, slid down the ice-house roof and romped with the dogs.

"Little Willie was more than happy with old Sally.

" 'What has become of Ann B——' Mary asked mother. 'We quarreled when we were children. Ann thought President Jackson was better looking than Henry Clay and my father both rolled into one and I threatened that after the election General Jackson would never smile again. Poor General Jackson! His smiles indeed were very rare after his political victory. To lose his beautiful wife! He adored her and was so overcome with grief as she was lowered gently into her grave in the garden of roses they both had loved and tended, that he had to be supported in the arms of a friend to enable him to stand upright. What agony to go straight from the grave of all he held dear to be reinstated as President! What was victory then? A dead sea apple full of luscious promise outside, and inside nothing but dull, bitter gray ashes.

" 'I also,' said Emilie, 'had a quarrel about Mr. Clay—when he was running for President against Mr. Polk. Father had brought me from New Orleans the most beautiful doll I have ever seen. Katherine B—— and I were playing with it, and she said, 'I bet you your doll that Mr. Polk will be elected.' I lost the bet and Katherine came to claim the doll. I refused to give it to her and we were having high and angry words when father hearing us came into the room to see what the trouble was.

"Katherine told him of our bet. Father said, 'Emilie, is that true?' I nodded my head in dumb agony. 'Then,' said father gently 'you must give Katherine your doll; it is highly dishonorable not to pay your debts.' Katherine went off triumphantly hugging my lovely doll, and I threw myself into father's arms in a convulsion of grief. I haven't yet forgiven Katherine,' said Emilie, laughing. 'If Emilie cherishes bitterness in this way, she will grow to be like our old friend Maria ——' said Mrs. Todd to Mary.

"Maria's husband, as you remember, was very cross and tyrannical to her. In order to make amends for some particular piece of tyranny and to gratify his own inordinate vanity, he ordered a marble bust of himself to present to his wife, but he died before it was sent home. His widow burst into tears when she saw it, 'Oh, Sugar, Sugar, my poor, poor Sugar,' she wept, 'your very living image! take that, and that, and that!' she cried angrily, slapping the marble face, first on one cheek and then on the other, in a sudden revulsion of feeling. 'She derives great satisfaction,' smiled Mrs. Todd, 'from the possession of that marble bust, though her hands are not as soft as they used to be.' Sister Mary smiled at this gossip of their friends and acquaintances, though much of the time she was very sad, grieving for her little dead baby and for our father.

"After Sister Mary left Kentucky, I counted the days until I could accept her invitation to make her a visit, and finally, when I was about eighteen, I set out happily for Illinois to visit my four sisters. Ann Todd was now married to Mr. C. M. Smith. It was in December when I arrived, and Springfield was in the midst of a whirl of gayety; parties and balls followed each other in quick succession; and Sister Mary was very gay that winter. I was struck with her exquisite taste in dress. One gown, I remember, was a lovely lavender brocade which she had made herself, and which she wore with a round point lace collar. Our sister Mrs. Edwards entertained several times that winter, as did also Mr. and Mrs. Ben Edwards.

"Mr. and Mrs. Lincoln went to a large party at the Ridgleys leaving everything apparently secure at home with a maid to watch the children. The party was very delightful, but Mary grew restless and anxious, and finally said 'Mr. Lincoln, we must go home.' (Mary never called her husband by his first name, Abraham or Abr'am, but always formally 'Mr. Lincoln.' I never heard her speak to him in any other way except in talking to her children, when she would say, 'Father said' thus and so.) 'We *must* go home, Mr. Lincoln,' she repeated, but he was reluctant and suggested that they stay a while longer. She insisted, however, that she must go and told him she would get someone to take her home that he might stay and enjoy himself. With his unfailing kindness, he said, 'I will take you home. We will find everything all right and then we can come back and enjoy the rest of the evening.' They did not come back, however, as they found the house on fire, the maid fast asleep, and the children's lives in danger. Mr. Lincoln said he was glad he had a wife who could 'sniff fire a quarter of a mile away.'

"Mary seemed almost clairvoyant, her intuitions were so clear and strong. She insisted that Mr. Lincoln should not take the position of provisional governor of Oregon. If he had taken it, his chance of being made President would have been destroyed.

"Governor Matteson had a beautiful daughter Lydia. Coming home from church one morning, my sister said to me, 'Emilie, you are just as pretty as Lydia, but I do not like your bonnet.' The next Sunday 'Little Sister's' head was crowned with a white velvet bonnet smothered in lovely white plumes, a gift from my sister and brother Lincoln.

"I was at the State House with my sister Mrs. Edwards, when Trumbull was elected to the United States Senate. I remember how indignant we were that our man was not the chosen one. We feared it would be a terrible blow to Mary, but if she was disappointed she kept it strictly to herself. I saw Mary Lincoln every day during my six months' visit to Springfield. We often went for long drives beyond the limits of the town and Bob, who was quite a little Chesterfield, due to his mother's careful training, would help us out of the carriage and we would gather wild flowers and carry home great armfuls.

"Mary was reading the novels and poems of Sir Walter Scott to Bob that spring. One day hearing sounds of strife, we ran to the window. Bob and a playmate were having a battle royal. Bob, with his sturdy little legs wide apart, was wielding a fence paling in lieu of a lance and proclaiming in a loud voice, 'This rock shall fly from its firm base as soon as I.' Mary, bubbling with laughter, called out 'Gramercy, brave knights. Pray be more merciful than you are brawny.'

"Mary enjoyed reading a wide range of subjects, often reviewing a book for Mr. Lincoln. I heard him say he had no need to read a book after Mary gave him a synopsis. He had great respect for her judgment and never took an important step without consulting her.

"Mr. Lincoln appealed to the eternal feminine in Mary. She mothered her husband as she did her children, and he seemed very dependent on her. She would call him back and make him wrap his throat in a muffler. She watched his health as she did that of her little sons, and he never sccmed impatient over all this fuss made over him. She was full of coquetry, and often patted his arm and slipped her lovely little white hand into his. The contrast between his big, bony, brown hand and hers was almost ludicrous. She was noted for her lovely hands. They were well formed, and as white as the roses she so often wore in her hair. She must have known how pretty her hands were for she made many quick little waves and bird-like gestures with them as she talked.

"Sister Elizabeth [Mrs. Ninian Edwards] had invited all of us to a supper party. Sister Mary had just finished a new dress, it was a white silk with blue brocaded flowers scattered over it in bunches and little garlands. When Mr. Lincoln came from his office Mary reminded him it was time to change for the party. He looked at her with a smile. 'Fine feathers enough on you to make fine birds of both of us.' Noticing her dress still further, he said, 'Those posies on your dress are the color of your eyes.' Mary dimpled with pleasure: 'You see, Emilie, I am training my husband to see color. I do not think he knew pink from blue when I married him.'

"One evening Bob and I were playing checkers. Mr. Lincoln was looking thoughtfully into the fire and apparently did not hear what Mary was saying. Finally a silence. Mary put down her piece of embroidery and said, 'Your silence is remarkably soothing, Mr. Lincoln, but we are not quite ready for sleep just yet.' As Mr. Lincoln did not seem to hear, Mary got up and took his hand, 'I fear my husband has become stone deaf since he left home at noon,' she said. 'I believe I have been both deaf and dumb for the last half hour,' replied Mr. Lincoln, 'but now you shall not complain'; and he launched into an anecdote of one of his clients which broke up the game of checkers and left us all speechless with laughter. Mary often watched for her husband and when it grew time for him to come home she would meet him at the gate and they would walk to the front door swinging hands and joking like two children.

"Any one could see that Mr. Lincoln admired Mary and was very proud of her. She took infinite pains to fascinate him again and again with pretty coquettish clothes and dainty little airs and graces. She was gay and light-hearted, hopeful and happy. She had a high temper and perhaps did not always have it under complete control, but what did it matter? Her little temper was soon over, and her husband loved her none the less, perhaps all the more, for this human frailty which needed his love and patience to pet and coax the sunny smile to replace the sarcasm and tears—and, oh, how she did love this man!

"She had a strong belief in predestination, ingrained in the blood of our Scottish Presbyterian ancestors, but wishing for any thing did not mean that she should not use an active brain and determined will to gain her end. She believed in prayer, but not a passive acceptance of fate if she could divert predestination into more pleasant channels. She said to me one day, 'What is to be is to be and nothing we can say, or do, or be can divert an inexorable fate, but in spite of knowing this, one feels better even after losing, if one has had a brave, whole-hearted fight to get the better of destiny.'

"Sister Mary asked me if our old nurse still believed that the jay birds went to hell every Friday night. When I answered, 'yes, indeed,' she turned to Brother Lincoln, saying: 'I am sure I have never told you how we were trained to be so prim and pious.' Pointing her finger at Brother Lincoln and mimicking Mammy's half-cajoling, half-reproving voice she threatened him: 'Nem mine, Mr. Jay's gitten so plum full of tales of you-alls devil*ment,* I'm feared he'll bust befo' Friday night an' time-come fur him to trabble to the bad place. Ole man Satan's done got the latch pulled, caze he

keeps track of the time an' when Mr. Jay pecks three
times, the do' flies open. But po' Mr. Jay is so weighten
down with the heavy burden of you-all's sins which he's
been totin' roun' all week that he can scacely fly up
to old man Satan's years which is just like a mule's, long
and hairy an' made plenty big on puppus so he won't
have the year-ache when Mr. Jay gets shet of his load.'
Brother Lincoln was highly amused and laughed heartily over Sister's impersonation.

"The next evening he was very late for supper and
the impatient cook (they had only the one maid) came
several times to the door to see if he had come. Finally,
two hours after the time set for the meal, in sauntered
Brother Lincoln as innocent as a lamb of any infraction
of domestic routine. Sister reminded him of the time
and said, 'I am afraid the chickens are burned to a
crisp.' Bob and I frankly said we were hungry. As
we sat down at the table, Brother Lincoln with a quiz-
zical smile said, pointing his finger at Sister, 'Nem
mine! Mr. Jay's gwine tell ole man Satan that Mary
sets her hungry husband down to burned up vittals just
caze he's two minutes late.' 'Two minutes!' we cried
in unison; 'two hours you mean.' 'Nem mine,' said
Brother Lincoln, 'just bring on the cinders and see how
quickly they will disappear.'

"I heard a story going the rounds of our family in

Springfield, told with variations and great glee to tease Mary, that Mr. Lincoln playing with the baby and pretending to be the pony pulling the baby-wagon forgot the baby in it and thinking of something else did not realize that he was pulling an empty wagon, that he had dumped the little driver, who was left kicking and squalling in the gutter.   Mary coming up the street at that moment, seeing the catastrophe, screamed and ran to the little fellow's assistance—and, who could blame her if she said a sharp word to the father so immersed in thought that he did not know he had spilled his baby?   With much laughter, they told me that Mr. Lincoln did not wait to hear all that Mary had to say, his long legs taking him out of sight with great celerity.

"Mr. Lincoln enjoyed his home and he and Mary idolized their children.   So far as I could see there was complete harmony and loving kindness between Mary and her husband, consideration for each other's wishes and a taste for the same books.   They seemed congenial in all things."

Mrs. Wallace, another sister, in speaking of the Lincolns, said, "Mary fairly worshipped him.   The story of their unhappiness is absolutely false."

Of course, the domestic machinery did not always run smoothly, and Mary, like most other housekeepers, had sometimes her problems with ignorant and inefficient servants, but those problems were hers alone to solve and did not give her the serious worry and anxiety she felt in regard to what she considered was vital to the best interests of her husband.

She felt that Herndon was detrimental to him and urged him to form a more desirable partnership. She had a keen, almost an uncanny, insight into the motives of men. She seemed able to penetrate the outer shell and to see clearly into the mind and soul of the person under her scrutiny. She distrusted Herndon and she did not believe in the sincerity of his friendship for her husband. The type of this man was abhorrent to Mary, and, honest above all things, she could not conceal her distaste for him, nor her horror for his very unfortunate habits, thereby incurring his bitter enmity. Her intuitions were fully justified when Herndon became a Lincoln historian.

Mary was full of fun and an airy sort of badinage, very puzzling to a dull-witted person. She is quoted as saying early in her married life, "Mr. Lincoln is not pretty; he would certainly make a magnificent President." Of course only a stupid person would take this as a serious prophecy, though, no doubt, she thought her husband better fitted to occupy that position than any other man in the world—for her faith in him was unbounded.

Mary Lincoln, while a painstaking and exquisite housekeeper, was so careful with her expenditures that Mr. Lincoln could help his own family and pay off the debt of the store at New Salem, which had failed before his marriage. She adored her children, and it was a pleasure to her to clothe their little bodies in garments of her own handiwork. She taught them, read aloud to them. There were now three noisy, enterprising boys to entertain, to keep out of mischief, although their pranks never seemed to annoy their mother and seemed deeply to interest their father who, joining in their romps, called them pet names.

Tad (Thomas), born April 4, 1853, his father nicknamed "Tadpole" when a baby because the little fellow's head seemed larger than usual and the abbreviation, "Tad," clung to him all his life.

Mr. Lincoln never interfered in the management of the children nor with Mary's domestic arrangements. Mary chided him for coming home in the rain without an umbrella; she was fearful about his health, which her brother-in-law, Dr. Wallace, had warned her to watch. She wanted to see him looking his best and was pleased when he wore broadcloth and a glossy tall silk hat. She shrank from any criticism of him and tried to make him more conventional. She did not want him to answer the door-bell and, when a member of her family said, "Mary, if I had a husband with a mind such as yours has, I would not care what he did," she was very much pleased, and answered, "It is foolish; a very small thing to complain of."

She was inordinately proud of him and believed in him with every fiber of her being. She longed for his success with all her heart because she wished the whole world to see him with her eyes, a great and glorious human being, the master spirit of his day and generation. She was thrilled as she saw his greatness being more and more recognized by his fellow citizens.

While her life was filled with love and home duties, she still found time to read; she kept in touch with current events and could forecast many a political outcome; she sympathized in all the political aims of her husband, advising him with far-seeing judgment when he turned to her for encouragement. They went to church together on Sunday, and she felt the "poetry" in his religious nature.

Mary, although a dyed-in-the-wool Presbyterian at the time she came to Springfield, as the guest of her sister Elizabeth, she, naturally, accompanied her hostess to church. Elizabeth, like Mary, had been brought up on the Shorter Catechism but had been con-

ROBERT SMITH TODD, MARY TODD'S FATHER
From an oil portrait painted by a Philadelphia artist about 1836

MRS. ROBERT S. TODD, MARY TODD LINCOLN'S STEP-
MOTHER

A miniature painted on ivory by Dodge about 1830, now
in the possession of the author

MRS. ALEXANDER HUMPHREYS, MARY TODD'S STEP-
GRANDMOTHER

From a painting by Mathew T. Jouett

firmed in the Episcopal church at the time of her marriage to Ninian Edwards, who was an Episcopalian. Mary, having formed her church affiliations which were the same as those of her sister, continued to attend service in the Episcopal church until after the death of her little son, Edward Baker, February 20, 1850. At that time, to quote a letter from Mary's cousin John Todd Stuart to the Reverend J. A. Reed:

"Dr. Smith, then pastor of the First Presbyterian Church of Springfield, at the suggestion of a lady friend of theirs, called upon Mr. and Mrs. Lincoln and that first visit resulted in great intimacy and friendship between them, lasting until the death of Mr. Lincoln and continuing with Mrs. Lincoln until the death of Dr. Smith. . . . I stated however that it was certainly true that up to that time Mr. Lincoln had never regularly attended any place of religious worship, but that after that he rented a pew in the First Presbyterian Church, and that his family constantly attended the worship in that church until he went to Washington as President. This much I said at that time and can now add that the Hon. Ninian Edwards, the brother-in-law of Mr. Lincoln, had within a few days informed me that when Mr. Lincoln commenced attending the Presbyterian Church, he admitted to him that his views had undergone the change claimed by Dr. Smith. I would further say that Dr. Smith was a man of very great ability and that on theological and metaphysical subjects, had few superiors and not many equals. Truthfulness was a prominent trait in

Mr. Lincoln's character and it would be impossible for any intimate friend of his to believe that he ever aimed to deceive either by his words or conduct.

"Yours truly,

JOHN T. STUART."

Mary kept up her French. Mr. Rankin says, in *Personal Recollections of Lincoln,* that in 1856, while sorting over magazines and pamphlets in Lincoln and Herndon's office, he came across in the *Southern Literary Messenger* a letter from their Paris correspondent giving a full translation of Victor Hugo's address on Capital Punishment. Knowing Mrs. Lincoln's fondness for French literature, he called at the Lincoln home with the magazine that she might read it. The address was Victor Hugo's defense of his son. The translation did not entirely satisfy Mrs. Lincoln and she insisted that a copy of the speech in French should be sent for. She thought some of the fire and feeling might have been lost in the English translation. As soon as the French copy came Mr. Rankin took it to her together with the translation of the Paris correspondent that he might follow the thought, while she read aloud the speech as delivered in French.

"She read with such sympathy that instead of following the English translation, I could only sit entranced by the force and effect of her tones as she translated or at times read Hugo's inspiring oration in his native language. She was an excellent reader and her sympathy with French was perfect." This incident occurred fourteen years after her marriage. She did not neglect her social duties—pleasures would be a more descriptive word,—for she loved parties. Amid brilliant lights, colorful costumes, flowers, music, and dancing, laughter and gay witty speech, she was in her element, charmed and charming. She sympathized warmly with Mr. Lincoln in his fondness for the theater, and they rarely missed a good company playing in Springfield. Her schoolmate Miss Bodley (afterwards Mrs. Owsley), who was with her for four years at Madame Mentelle's, says: "Mary took a great interest in school theatricals and always took a prominent part in them."

"That reminds me of my first thought when I heard that Mary had married a poor young lawyer in Springfield. Of course we girls at Madame Mentelle's used to discuss our future husbands, laying down the law pretty explicitly as to what they would have to be and what we should expect of them. Mary Todd stipulated that her choice should be willing and able to let her see as much of the theater as she wanted, and beyond that she did not expect to be too particular. So when I heard she had chosen a struggling young lawyer (the plainest looking man in Springfield, her sister wrote me), I wondered how she was going to manage about the theater-going."

While Mary was courageous and daring about most things, a thunderstorm was terrifying to her. Mr. Lincoln, knowing this, at the first muttering of thunder would leave his law office and hurry home to quiet her fears and comfort her until the storm was over.

Emilie Todd, Mary's sister, was now married to Ben Hardin Helm (son of Governor Helm of Kentucky), and Mary kept up a desultory correspondence with her. Mary was eighteen years older than Emilie, so in these letters she dwells on the gossip of the younger set, the parties and balls, the beaux and belles, the news that she thinks will be of greatest interest to her young sister, interspersed with family gossip and politics always interesting to Kentucky women from the cradle to the grave. These letters are not dated except in respect to the day of the month, but they probably came in the order named and were written in 1856 and 1857.

"Springfield,
February 16.

"Think not, dear Emilie, altho' weeks have passed since your welcome letter was received that you had been for-gotten or that I have not daily proposed writing you, yet something has always occurred to oppose my good resolu-tions. This winter has certainly passed most rapidly.

Spring, if we can call the month of March such, is nearly here. The first part of the winter was unusually quiet owing to so much sickness among children. With scarlet fever in several families some two or three children were swept away.

"Within the last three weeks there has been a party almost every night and some two or three grand fêtes are coming off this week. I may perhaps surprise you when I mention that I am recovering from the slight fatigue of a very large and I really believe a very handsome entertainment, at least our friends flatter us by saying so. About five hundred were invited, yet owing to an unlucky rain three hundred only favored us by their presence and the same evening in Jacksonville, Colonel Warren gave a bridal party to his son who married Miss Birchall of this place which occasion robbed us of some of our friends. You will think we have enlarged our borders since you were here. Three evenings since, Governor Bissell gave a very large party, I thought of you frequently that evening when I saw so many of your acquaintances beautifully dressed and dancing away very happily and as enquiries were made about you during the evening by both beaux and belles you could not fail to be remembered. I wish you would write me more frequently and tell me all about yourself. You have so much leisure and such a literary husband that you will become a regular blue. Your old laugh will soften the solemnity of such a character and the old Emilie of former times will show herself. Miss Dunlap is spending the winter with her sister Mrs. Mc looking very pretty but the beaux do not appear so numerous as the winter you passed here. Within the last two or three weeks I have often wished that Dedee[1] was here, yet the first part of the winter was so quiet that I feared she would not have enjoyed herself. I hope another winter both Kitty[2] and Dedee will come out and we will endeavor to make it as pleasant as possible for them.

"Dr. and Mrs. Brown also Mr. Dwight Brown and his wife, are residing here. The former has charge of the First Church, whether the arrangement will suit all around remains to be proven. I must hasten to conclude as I am interrupted by company. Hoping to be remembered to your husband, I remain

Yours truly,
MARY LINCOLN."

"Springfield,
September 20.

"My dear Emilie:

"So long a time has passed since your last letter that I scarcely know how to ask you to excuse my silence . . . I only pray you to return good for evil and let me hear from you more frequently. Do write me all the news, I feel anxious to hear from you. The summer has so strangely and rapidly passed away. Some portion of it was spent most pleasantly in traveling East. We visited Niagara,

[1] Elodie Todd, younger sister.
[2] Katherine Bodley Todd, youngest of the Todd sisters.

1856

Springfield. Nov 23ᵈ

        With much pleasure, my dear
Emilie, I acknowledge, the reciept
of one of your ever acceptable let-
-ters, & notwithstanding many
weeks have passed, since writing
you, I have frequently intended
doing so, & you have been often-
-times in my thoughts. Mr E-
expressed great pleasure at meet-
-ing you last summer, you
know you have a very warm
place in his heart, You have been
such a wanderer around with
your good husband, and a letter
might have failed reaching you

FACSIMILE OF LETTER TO HER SISTER

I saw Elizabeth, this afternoon. Julia & Mr
Baker are in Peoria, at the fair, from
thence go to St Louis – At the county fair,
here last week, Julia's, last quilt (which
makes her third one) a very handsome
silk one, took the premium she tries for
the like fate at Peoria & St Louis; she has
nothing but her dear Husband & Silk
quilts, to occupy her time – How, different the daily routine of some of
our lives are – It is getting very late,
dear Emilie, and I must close, my little
billet – Shall I apologise for this scrawl
I know, I ought to be ashamed of it.
When you read this, like a good sister,
sit down & write me a good long letter,
all about yourself – Mr L – is not at home
this makes the fourth week, he has been in
Chicago. Remember me to your Husband.
Yours affectionately
Mary L

FACSIMILE OF LETTER TO HER SISTER

Canada, New York and other points of interest. When I saw the large steamers at the New York landings I felt in my heart inclined to sigh that poverty was my portion. How I long to go to Europe I often laugh and tell Mr. Lincoln that I am determined my next husband shall be rich.

"You can scarcely imagine a place improving more rapidly than ours. Almost palaces of homes have been reared since you were here, hundreds of houses have been going up this season and some of them very elegant. Governor Matteson's house is just being completed, the whole place has cost him, he says, $100,000. but he is now worth a million. I saw Elizabeth[1] this afternoon. Julia and Mr. Baker[2] are in Peoria at the fair, from thence go to St. Louis. At the County fair here last week Julia's last quilt (which makes her third one) is a very handsome silk one, took the premium. She trusts for the like fate at Peoria and St. Louis. She has nothing but her dear husband and silk quilts to occupy her time. How different the daily routine of some of our lives. It is getting very late dear Emilie and I must close my little billet. Shall I apologize for this scrawl? I know I ought to be ashamed of it. When you read this sit down and like a good little sister write me a good long letter all about yourself. Mr. Lincoln is not at home. This makes the third week he has been in Chicago.

"Yours affectionately,

MARY L."

[1] Her sister Mrs. Ninian Edwards.
[2] Mrs. Edwards' daughter and son-in-law.

"Springfield,
November 23.

With much pleasure, my dear Emilie, I acknowledge the
receipt of one of your ever acceptable letters, and notwithstanding many weeks have passed since writing you, I have
frequently intended doing so and you have been often in
my thoughts.   Mr. Edwards [1] expressed great pleasure at
meeting you last summer.   You know you have a very
warm place in his heart.   You have been such a wanderer
around with your good husband and a letter might have
failed to reach you.   I must try to devise some excuses for
my past silence, forgetfulness you know it could not be.
Besides there is a great deal in getting out of the habit of
letter writing; once I was very fond of it.   Nothing pleases
me better than to receive a letter from an absent friend, so
remember dear Emilie, when you desire to be particularly
acceptable, write me one of your agreeable missives and do
not wait for a return of each from a staid matron and
moreover the mother of three noisy boys.   Your husband
like some of the rest of ours has a great taste for politics
and has taken much interest in the late contest which has
resulted very much as I expected, not hoped, although
Mr. Lincoln is or was a Fremont man, you must not include
him with so many of those who belong to that party, an
Abolitionist.   In principle he is far from it, all he desires
is that slavery shall not be extended, let it remain where it
is.   My weak woman's heart was too Southern in feeling
to sympathize with any but Filmore.   I have always been

[1] Ninian Edwards, brother-in-law.

his great admirer; he made so good a President and is so just a man and feels the necessity of keeping the foreigners within bounds. If some of you Kentuckians had to deal with the "Wild Irish" as we housekeepers are some times called upon to do, the South would certainly elect Mr. Filmore next time. The Democrats in our State have been defeated in their Governor so there is a crumb of comfort for each and all. What day is so dark that there is no ray of sunshine to penetrate the gloom? Speaking of politics, Governors, etc., reminds me of your questions relative to Lydia M. The hour of her patient lover's deliverance is at hand, they are to be married privately I expect. Some of us who had a handsome dress for the season thought it would be in good taste for Mrs. Matteson in consideration of their being about to leave their present habitation to give a general reception. Lydia has always been so retiring that she would be very averse to a public display. This fall in visiting Mrs. M. I met a sister of Mrs. McGinnis, a very pretty well bred woman from Joliet, she spoke of having met Margaret Kellogg[1] in Kentucky. Frances Wallace[2] returned two or three days ago from her visit to Pennsylvania where she has been spending the fall. Mr. Edwards' family are well. Mr. Baker and Julia[3] are still with them. Miss Iles was married some three weeks since (I expect you do not remember her) which gave rise to some two or three parties. Mr. Scott is fre-

[1] Margaret Todd Kellogg, sister of Mrs. Lincoln.
[2] Frances Todd, another sister.
[3] Julia Edwards Baker, daughter of Ninian Edwards.

quently here rather playing the devoted to Julia.[1] I suspect, whether anything serious I do not know, the family would not be averse to him. Charley R. was on a visit to him in Lexington. He, it is said, is to be married this winter to Jennie Barrett, a lovely girl, you remember her.

"I am sorry to hear that dear mother is frequently indisposed. I hope she has recovered from her lameness. Tell her when you see her that our old acquaintance Mr. ——— took tea with us an evening or two since and made particular enquiries about her. Still as rough and uncultivated as ever although some years since married an accomplished Georgia belle with the advantages of some winters in Washington. Mother and I when last together spoke of our Minister, Mr. Smith, who finding his salary of some $1600 inadequate has resigned the Church. Uncle and some few others are desirous of getting Dr. Brown your former pastor in Lexington. Within the last year both he and his wife have been a great deal here. He has purchased land and appears rather identified with the Country.

"But I am speaking of things that will not interest you in the least. If you do not bring yourself and your husband to see us very soon we will think you are not as proud of him as rumor says you should be. Do write soon in return for this long and I fear dull letter from yours truly,

MARY LINCOLN."

In 1857 Ben Hardin Helm (Mary Lincoln's brother-in-law) had occasion to go to Springfield to argue a

[1] Do not know what Julia she refers to, but not a member of her family.

law case. He promptly called on the Lincolns with many messages from "Little Sister." Mary, with warm cordiality, held out both hands to him, and turning impulsively to Mr. Lincoln, said, "So this tall young Kentuckian is Little Sister's husband; he shall have a double welcome as a Kentuckian and as a brother." "And also as the grandson of the Kitchen Knife Whetted on a Brick," added Mr. Lincoln. "Well," said Mary to Helm, "in spite of the fact that the speech in Congress which fastened that soubriquet on your grandfather, Mr. Ben Hardin, was made against our political idol, Mr. Clay, I have always had a sincere admiration for your grandfather's ability to cut roughly but cut deep."

Mr. Lincoln quietly slipped out of the room and sent to the hotel for Helm's luggage, insisting that he must make their house his home while in Springfield.

Helm spent a delightful week with them and he and his brother-in-law formed a friendship which was more like the affection of brothers than the ordinary liking of men. Lincoln and his young brother-in-law had much of mutual interest to talk about. Lincoln's father (Thomas Lincoln) had settled in Elizabethtown, Hardin county, Kentucky, and there had plied his trade of cabinet-maker and carpenter before he bought his farm near Hodgenville, about ten miles from Elizabethtown, where Lincoln was born. Helm's father owned a large body of land one mile from Elizabethtown. While Helm was twenty-three years younger than Lincoln, he had all of the traditions of Hardin county at his finger tips and could answer Lincoln's interested questions.

Lincoln, Helm, and Mary animatedly discussed the political situation. Both Helm and Mary came of slave-owning people who personally had never seen cruelty practiced, who both had been nursed by loving black mammies whose word was law and must be obeyed implicitly by the children under her charge.

Helm feared the freeing of the slaves would ruin the South. Mary agreed with her husband that the institution of slavery was a blot on the country. Neither at that time dreamed of sudden emancipation. Lincoln and Helm realized and deeply deplored the bitterness and hatred growing up between the two sections of the country. While Lincoln was a Republican and Helm a Southern-rights Democrat, they were thoughtful, conservative men; both were born in the same State, within a few miles of each other; both had a full understanding of the conditions and prejudices of the Southern people.

Lincoln declared, "They are just what we would be in their situation. If slavery did not exist among them, they would not introduce it. If it did now exist among us, we should not instantly give it up. I surely will not blame them for not doing what I should not know how to do myself. If all earthly power were given me, I should not know what to do as to the existing institution. My first impulse would be to free all the slaves and send them to Liberia to their own native land. But a moment's reflection would convince me that . . . its sudden execution is impossible, etc."

"I regret as you do," said Helm to Lincoln, "that the importation of slaves into the South was ever allowed but we must realize that under the guarantees of the Constitution an immense amount of wealth in the Southern States has been wrapt up in slaves, indeed, slaves must constitute nearly half of all the property owned in the South." "But," cried Mary, "this rich government would compensate the owners for their slaves and in time send the negroes back to their native land." "No," said Helm, "the Northern Abolitionists will never consent to that plan. They have already declared it would be a disgrace to the nation to pay for emancipated slaves. The South bought the slaves in good faith,"—he laughed, "most people have a fancy for holding on to their property even," he added gravely, "if much trouble comes of it."

Lincoln reminded Helm that the Abolitionists were

a comparatively small body of extremists and so did not represent Northern opinion. He believed that compensated emancipation would be accepted at least by the Border States. "Never by the Cotton States," cried Helm, who had traveled among them. "They insist upon their Constitutional rights and independence of Federal power where they are concerned."

Helm and Mr. Lincoln were very congenial; though differing in politics, their ideas of law, philosophy, and serious aims in life brought them very close together. Mary and Mr. Lincoln treated their young brother-in-law with so much kindness and affection and consideration that he felt they had indeed accepted him as a brother. And for Mary, who had taken him so warm-heartedly into her home and heart on his own account, as well as Emilie's, he had nothing but praise.

It was a visit that he constantly recalled to his wife with the greatest pleasure. Mrs. Lincoln was his ideal of a hostess, and Mr. Lincoln an earnest, high-minded statesman. Helm often spoke of Mr. Lincoln's seriousness, saying that in their talks together he had not told a single anecdote or joke such as he was credited with uttering on almost every occasion.

CHAPTER VII

WASHINGTON LOOMS

AT THE end of his single term in Congress in 1849, Abraham Lincoln retired permanently, as he thought, from politics; for five years thereafter he devoted his time and talents to the practice of law.

He and Mary during this time read and studied much together. They were both fully abreast of the times in the world of politics. Newspapers and editorials were alive and exciting. The repeal of the Missouri Compromise in May, 1854, put through by the Democrats under the leadership of Lincoln's inveterate political rival Stephen A. Douglas, stirred Lincoln and Mary to the very core, and Lincoln was spurred into immediate action. He returned to political life and helped to form the Republican party. The old Whig party, which had avoided making an issue of the slavery question, now gave a last expiring gasp and the former Whigs in the North united with those Democrats and Free Soilers having anti-slavery principles. Many of them were not Abolitionists. They were united on the firm platform that slavery should not be extended.

Hot heads now, both North and South, were threatening the country with disunion. There was no epithet too insulting for the North to fling at the South, and the South flamed with answering vituperation of the North; each section inflaming the passions of the other day by day with more bitter hatred. The founders of the Republic and the Holy Scriptures were appealed to by ardent partisans on both sides of the question. The press, politicians, authors, ministers of the gospel, all played their part. To quote a few:

The *Boston Liberator,* January 11, 1855, contained this statement: "Mr. Giddings [1] says truly that the dissolution of the Union has long been held up as a scarecrow by the South; but when he adds that the friends of liberty have never demanded it, his statement is untrue unless he means to confine it to his political associates who are but compromisers at best. We demand nothing short of a dissolution, absolute and immediate. . . . At the twenty-third annual meeting of the Massachusetts Anti-Slavery Society, which convened at Boston on the 24th of January, 1856, it was

"Resolved, that the one great issue before the country is the dissolution of the Union in comparison with which all other issues with the slave power are as dust in the balance. Therefore, we will give ourselves to the work of annulling this covenant with death, as

[1] Joshua R. Giddings of Ohio.

SEAL OWNED AND USED BY MRS. ALEXANDER HUMPHREYS, MARY TODD'S
STEPGRANDMOTHER

The handle is amethyst, the wheel gold, containing six seals—congratulation, greeting, farewell, condolence, friendship neglected, and monogram

HOME OF ROBERT S. TODD ON MAIN STREET, LEXINGTON, KENTUCKY

Long since given up to commercial uses, it has fallen sadly from its once desirable estate. At the left of the house there was a conservatory opening from the library into a large formal flower garden covering the entire block. There for eight years of Mary Todd's life she played and studied and gathered roses to tuck coquettishly in her chestnut curls

MRS. NINIAN EDWARDS

Mary Todd's sister Elizabeth, at whose home in Springfield, Illinois, she
was married to Abraham Lincoln; from the same home she was borne to her
last resting-place by the side of her husband

essential to our own innocency and the speedy and ever-lasting overthrow of the slave system."

Wendell Philips, on that occasion, spoke in favor of disunion: "I entirely accord with the sentiment of the last resolution. I think all we have to do is to prepare the public mind by the daily and hourly presentation of the doctrine of disunion."

On the Fourth of July, 1856, at a mass meeting held at Farmington, Massachusetts, several disunion speeches were made. William Lloyd Garrison said, "Let us then to-day, rejecting as wild and chimerical all suggestions and contrivances and propositions for restraining slavery in its present limits, while extending protection to it in fifteen of the thirty-one States, register our pledge anew before Heaven and the World that we will do what in us lies to effect the eternal overthrow of this blood-stained Union, that our enslaved countrymen may find a sure deliverance, and we may no longer be answerable for their blood."

J. B. Swansey then addressed the meeting and wound up his speech by saying, "I believe that the duty of every true man is now to take the ground of secession."

Horace Greeley, editor of the New York *Tribune* and as such, one of the leaders of the disunion party in the North, said, "The Union is not worth supporting in connection with the South."

N. P. Banks, governor of Massachusetts, said, "I am willing in a certain state of circumstances to let the Union slide."

Rufus Spaulding declared, "In the case of the alternative being presented, of the continuance of slavery or a dissolution of the Union, I am for dissolution and I care not how soon it comes."

A leading Republican newspaper during the campaign of 1856 when John C. Frémont was the standard bearer, of the new party, bore the motto in headlines, "No Union with slave holders! The United States Constitution is a covenant with death and an agreement with Hell!"

Joshua R. Giddings, member of Congress, said: "I look forward to the day when there shall be a servile insurrection in the South; when the black man armed with British bayonets and led by British officers shall assert his freedom, and wage a war of extermination against his master. When the torch of the incendiary shall light up the towns and cities of the South and blot out the last vestige of slavery. And though I may not laugh at their calamity, nor mock when their fear cometh, yet, I shall hail it as the dawn of a political millennium."

And while hatred flourished in the North and it was no better in the South, the South asserted, "Garrison and Phillips are undoubtedly right, and as honest as they are right when they pronounce the Constitution 'pro-slavery'; it is pro-slavery and, therefore, they curse it, and curse the Union of which it is the bond."

The South claimed that the North, after finding slave labor unsuited to the Northern climate, had disposed of her slaves to the South, instead of freeing them; that now, no longer burdened with slaves, Northerners had a suddenly awakened conscience as to the iniquity of the slave-owning tyrants to whom they had sold their slaves, and whose money they were jingling in their pockets from their profitable trade. The South claimed that the North feared that by the extension of slavery into newly admitted territory the South would have a preponderance of votes in Congress and the Senate, and therefore the balance of power in the Union.

The Northern fanatics quoted the Bible in support of their arguments against slavery. The Southern fanatics found just as many passages in the Bible to justify them in the possession of slaves. There were, however, conservative men on both sides who were willing and anxious to make compromises to save the Union intact.

Horatio Seymour, of New York, said: "When our fathers, on common battlefields were struggling for common rights, slavery existed in all our colonies; there was no exception; it was on every rood of ground. We had no difficulty on account of slavery, then, in achieving our independence, but since then slavery has been abolished over more than one-half of this land of ours. It is now in comparatively contracted limits, and now we hear that it must lead to alienation, or the disruption of this great confederacy. I fear we of the North are unjust, and not altogether courageous, in our treatment of our brethren of the South. How came slavery in these United States? Who brought the Negro from Africa? The South never had ships. The men of New York, where I came from, the men of Massachusetts and the men of Rhode Island were those who stole them from their homes and brought them over to the shambles here. . . .

"When the Constitution of the United States was formed and when the delegates from the different States met in convention, the question of slavery was there and it was asked when shall the slave trade be put an end to? Georgia said, Now. Virginia said, Now. South Carolina said, Not yet. Connecticut, Not yet, Rhode Island, Not yet, Massachusetts, Not yet, New Hampshire said, Not yet, the slave trade is profitable. If you will read Minot's *History of Massachusetts* you will learn that the great business of New England was at one time the manufacture of rum, pure rum, and when they made rum, they took it to the coast of Africa and exchanged it for slaves. The slavers landed their cargoes on some unfrequented shores of the Southern coast, and forthwith the entire South was charged with complicity in the slave trade."

Lincoln was called half-hearted in the North because he persisted in his belief in the rights of the Slave States guaranteed by the Constitution. His principal aim in life now was to save the Union if he could. "If I could save the Union by emancipating all the slaves, I would do so; if I could save it by emancipating none of them, I would do it; if I could save it by emancipating some and not others, I would do that too." Few men were as single in purpose and as unswerving as Lincoln to effect the preservation of the Union.

In 1857 the Republican party had, shortly after the inauguration of President Buchanan, received a staggering blow from a totally unexpected quarter when it was decided by Chief Justice Taney and a majority of the Judges of the Supreme Court of the United States that the exclusion of slavery from any part of the territories was unconstitutional, and in the Dred Scott case the Chief Justice and his associates decided that the negro, Dred Scott, was not a citizen and also not free, because the Missouri Compromise had always been

void and unconstitutional. Chief Justice Taney declared that the makers of the Constitution and the
authors of the Declaration of Independence had not
meant the negro when they used the words "man,"
"persons," "citizens." (In several states at that time,
free negroes were exercising the right to vote.) While
this opinion, coming as it did from the highest tribunal
in the land, confirmed the South in the legality of their
policy of slave-holding, it raised an angry storm of protest in the North. To be assured by the Supreme Court
of the United States that the platform of the Republican party was unconstitutional, filled them with furious
indignation. The Republicans were embarrassed and
deeply depressed.

The South jubilant that States' Rights had been vin-
dicated. The South had always feared a centralization
of government in the North as being sectional, and
last, but not least, property (slave or otherwise) owned
under the guarantees of the Constitution could not
legally be taken away without compensation and the
consent of the owner.

Mr. Lincoln, thoughtful and conservative, declared,
"And no matter what our grievance, even though
Kansas shall come in as a Slave State; and no matter
what theirs, even if we shall restore the Compromise
we will say to the Southern disunionists, we won't go

out of the Union and you shan't." This "you shan't"
the hot headed Southerners took to be a challenge.
Calmer Southerners, who were for preserving the
Union by some sort of compromise, were insulted and
called Abolitionists. The storm of protest raised in the
North by this decision of the Supreme Court caused
Judge Douglas to hasten to Illinois to calm his con-
stituents. Douglas was handsome, an orator, and had
great personal magnetism; he was already a brilliant
success and his party thought of him as good timber for
President of the United States, at no distant time.
"What," exclaimed Douglas, "oppose the Supreme
Court! Is it not sacred? To resist it is anarchy."
Mr. Lincoln answered this speech of Douglas with such
forcible arguments against the decision of the Judges
in the Dred Scott case that he appealed to the common
sense and fairness of his audiences and won the praise
of even the most radical leaders in the Republican
party.

Lincoln was growing more and more popular with
his party. In 1858 he and Douglas were opposing
candidates for United States senator from Illinois and,
as Douglas was rather evading the question of slavery
which was uppermost in Lincoln's mind, he challenged
Douglas to a series of joint debates in which he proposed to make Douglas come out in the open and de-

clare his real sentiments. Those debates are now famous in history.

Mary Lincoln urged her husband to pit his strength against Douglas, and when Lincoln was rather despondent and felt that the race of ambition had been a failure—a flat failure for him, and a splendid success for Douglas—Mary said with spirit, her head thrown back and her eyes shining with pride, "Mr. Douglas is a very little, *little* giant by the side of my tall Kentuckian, and intellectually my husband towers above Douglas just as he does physically." Mary's faith in her husband encouraged him and gave him more confidence in his own strength; for Mary had a wonderful and peculiar influence over this great man, and his confidence in her judgment was seldom at fault. Mary was filled with indignation when anyone presumed to say her husband was an Abolitionist, especially after Lincoln himself had repudiated such an idea. She read and applauded all of Lincoln's speeches in this debate. "How foolish," she cried, "for Douglas to think that because you demand justice for the negro you are in favor of abolition or that you would ever, in any event, countenance social equality with a race so far inferior to your own. He is insolent," she cried.

"There are many free negroes in the South and no thought in the minds of whites or blacks of social equal-

ity. Indeed," she laughed, "you should see the scorn
with which our servants speak of 'free niggers.' They
call themselves 'niggers'," she said, "but mother would
have punished any one of us for using that term." Mary
laughed as she quoted her stepmother: "'A mode of
speaking of the negro at once scornful and inelegant.'
Social equality, indeed!" she laughed.

"There is a natural disgust in the minds of nearly all
white people at the idea of an indiscriminate amalga-
mation of the white and black men," said Mr. Lincoln.
And in their political discussions he did not think it
must *necessarily* follow that in the event of emancipation, the negro must have full and equal political rights
with white men.

During the debates, the progress of Mr. Douglas was
like the triumphal procession of a conquering hero.
His special train of cars with flags flying, his band of
music, his bodyguard of devoted friends—he even had
a cannon to boom announcement of his approach to a
town where he was scheduled to speak. Mr. Douglas
was accompanied throughout this campaign by his wife,
a brilliant, beautiful woman.

It is said that Douglas spent no less than $50,000 in
this canvass. Mr. Lincoln, who thought that he had
been extravagant to spend five hundred dollars, traveled modestly, sometimes even on a caboose or freight

train, but as he hated "fireworks, fizzle gigs," this mode of travel suited him better. Mrs. Lincoln stayed quietly at home and kept the home fires burning, trained her children, and read accounts of the speeches in the papers.

In the Freeport debate, Mr. Lincoln, against the advice of his friends, asked Mr. Douglas, "Can the people of a United States territory in any lawful way, against the wish of any citizen of the United States, exclude slavery from its limits prior to the formation of a State constitution?" Douglas answered, "It matters not which way the Supreme Court may hereafter decide as to the abstract question whether slavery may or may not go into a territory under the Constitution, the people have the lawful means to introduce it or exclude it as they please, for the reason that slavery cannot exist a day or an hour anywhere unless it is supported by local police regulations. Those police regulations can only be established by the local legislature, and if the people are opposed to slavery, they will elect representatives to that body who will, by unfriendly legislation, effectually prevent the introduction of it in their midst. If on the contrary they are for it, their legislature will favor its extension."

Douglas thought he had by this answer satisfied all parties, and the Democrats congratulated him on his cleverness. But Lincoln, an astute politician, smiled and waited for the Southern press. The verdict came with no uncertain sound: Douglas was a traitor; he had repudiated the verdict of the Supreme Court. Douglas was now an impossible candidate, in the South, for the Presidency in 1860, although he had won the Senatorship.

Mr. Lincoln came home one evening looking rather disturbed. In reply to Mary's "What is worrying you?" (for she was quick to note his moods), he told her he had just had a conversation with his friend Mr. Fell, who wished him to be a candidate for President of the United States. Mary's little crooked smile deepened into a dimple. "Is that anything to worry about?" she asked. "What is the use of talking of me for the Presidency?" said Mr. Lincoln impatiently, "Whilst we have such men as Seward, Chase, and others, who are so much better known to the people, and whose names are so intimately associated with the principles of the Republican party. Everybody knows them; nobody scarcely, outside of Illinois, knows me."

"They soon will," said Mary. Her husband smiled at her persistence.

"Besides," he continued, "is it not, as a matter of justice, due to such men, who have carried this movement forward to its present status, in spite of fearful opposition, personal abuse, and hard names? I really think so."

"Oh," smiled Mary, "if abuse is all that is needed to earn the Presidency I think you have earned part of the price already."

Mr. Lincoln was amused—what an ambitious little wife he had!—but he shook his head, there was no chance. Why force himself? But Mary's inherited instinct from her Indian-fighting ancestors was fired at the prospect of battle, and battle was chance. Why not take the chance? There was everything to gain and nothing to lose. "I admit," said her husband, "that I am ambitious and would like to be President, but there is no such good luck in store for me as the Presidency of these United States."

"Oh," cried Mary, "how you underrate yourself! But,"—with a knowing little smile, she added—"you are the only person in the world who does. You often quote Burns. 'Oh wad some power the giftie gie *you* to see yoursel' as ithers see you,'" she paraphrased.

Mr. Lincoln persisted in his modest estimate of himself. "I must in all candor say I do not think myself fit for the Presidency." Mary laughed at him for thinking himself "not fit." "You've no equal in the United States," she declared. She really thought he had no equal in the world.

Politics became more engrossing to Mr. Lincoln, and more and more in Mary's heart grew the triumphant conviction of his strength. On February 27, 1860, Mr. Lincoln made the famous Cooper Institute speech in New York that electrified his party. Two months later, in April, at Springfield, it was "Resolved" by his fellow citizens that "Abraham Lincoln is our first choice for President of the United States. * * * We deem ourselves honored to be permitted to testify our personal knowledge in everyday life as friend and neighbors of his inestimable worth as a private citizen, his faithful and able discharge of every public trust committed to his care, and the extraordinary gifts and brilliant attainments which have not only made his name a household word in the Prairie State but also made him the proud peer of the ablest jurists, the wisest statesman, and the most eloquent orator in the Union."

Letters now came in a steady stream, some from totally unexpected quarters. Mary with quickened pulses realized what it meant. "Fit or not," she exclaimed, "you are in the field." Then with lowered voice solemn with prophecy, she declared, "You will be President of the United States." Her husband smilingly shook his head; of course, he did not attach any importance to this prophecy, which was the expression of Mary's unbounded love and ambition for him, and yet, it was strange how often Mary could see far into the political future—strange and unexpected things did happen—perhaps—— Mr. Lincoln was passively ambitious; Mary, keen for battle on the front line, feared no defeat in this conflict, had no thought that her man might, even with flying colors, go down in defeat.

The State Convention met at Decatur, May 9 and 10, 1860, and with wild enthusiasm unanimously declared for Lincoln as President. On May 16, the Republican Convention was formally opened in Chicago. When Mr. Norman B. Judd, of Illinois, nominated Lincoln, there was a great demonstration, the crowd cheered and clapped, the women waved handkerchiefs and flags. A moment later the seconding of William H. Seward's nomination was the signal for a still greater demonstration.

But when Caleb Smith, of Indiana, seconded the nomination of Lincoln such pandemonium was let loose as made the preceding noise seem a gentle murmur in comparison. In the first lull, Mary Lincoln's cousin, Stephen T. Logan, hoarse with screaming and beside himself with excitement, called out, "Mr. President, in order or out of order, I propose this convention and audience give three cheers for the man who is evidently their nominee."

The balloting was another strain. Illinois men thought they had a hundred votes; counting, they found they had 102. Pennsylvania had fifty and one-half votes; Chase, forty-nine; Greeley's men, forty-eight; McLean, Pennsylvania's second choice, twelve. It was for Pennsylvania to say whether Seward was to be defeated. The Pennsylvania delegation moved that on the second ballot Pennsylvania's vote be cast solidly for Lincoln. When Pennsylvania's name was called amid a profound silence, the multitude in the Wigwam heard the answer, "Pennsylvania casts her fifty-two votes for Abraham Lincoln." The third ballot Lincoln was distancing Seward—only two and a half more votes and Lincoln would have the nomination; there was an instant of breathless silence, and the chairman of the Ohio delegation, springing upon his chair cried, "I rise to change four votes from Mr. Chase to Mr. Lincoln."

The scene which followed baffles description. Men wept and sobbed on each other's shoulders, they threw hats, handkerchiefs, and canes in the air. It seemed as though they could not cease their expressions of joy; the tension had been so great and had lasted so long that these outbursts gave relief to pent up anxiety.

Mr. Lincoln and Mary all this time were in Springfield. They were feeling the tension and strain even more than their political friends in Chicago. Mr. Lincoln was restless and spent the weary waiting of this week drifting between the telegraph office and home, for Mary was anxious for every scrap of news. Mr. Lincoln was not as hopeful of the result as Mary. "Well," he said wearily, "I guess I'll go back to practicing law." "Why, of course," said Mary soothingly, "President Lincoln will return to Springfield and his law office in a few years, but he and Mrs. President are going to travel a little bit before they settle down to a quiet, humdrum life." How often they had talked and would still talk of their belated honeymoon trip! Friday morning both Mr. Lincoln and Mary had dark rings of fatigue and sleeplessness under their eyes, the suspense was almost unbearable, even their voices were strained and sounded unnatural as they tried to speak calmly and reassuringly to each other. Mr. Lincoln went to his office, but soon joined the excited throng around the telegraph office. His nomination came over the wire, then the balloting. The strain was too great, he would not wait. Remembering a commission Mary had given him that morning, he started across the square and was standing in the door of the shop when a shout went up from the group in front of the telegraph office.

"Lincoln is nominated!"

He was surrounded in an instant by an exultant crowd of half-hysterical friends bent on shaking his hand and shouting congratulations. The happy excitement of his friends was instantly reflected in Mr. Lincoln's beaming countenance, but realizing in a moment what it all meant, his face became very grave and thoughtful. He knew how serious was the crisis through which the country was passing and how great a responsibility the next President would have to assume.

"My friends," he said, "I am glad to receive your congratulations, and as there is a little woman on Eighth Street who will be glad to hear the news, you must excuse me until I inform her." He turned to Mary first for encouragement and for the triumphant love he knew he would find in her eyes. It does not take a very vivid imagination to picture their meeting: Lincoln proud of his wife and that he had realized her faith in his star, and Mary, her heart singing with joy over the honor that had come to her man—the father of her four sons,—her heart nearly bursting with the pride she felt in him.

There was not much sleep in Springfield that night for anyone, particularly Mary. The shouting and singing of campaign songs was sweet music, and the glowing, flaming bonfires and parades a beautiful sight, thrilling every nerve with exultation over the triumph of her loved one. Mary was not the only one exultant and happy. Her cousin Judge Stephen T. Logan, a grave and staid judge at all other times, had gone wild with excitement at Chicago, where he had headed the Convention. He had gone clad in the finest suit he had ever worn and "crowned with a tall new shiny silk hat." When he came back this suit, which he had not taken off since he left Springfield, was wrinkled and dusty and he was wearing a little Scotch cap—the tall silk hat having been beaten into a shapeless wreck over the shoulders of his happy fellow citizens. (From Rankin's *History*.)

CHAPTER VIII

INTO THE MISTS

FROM Friday, May 18, 1860, when Mr. Lincoln
was nominated for President of the United States
by the Republican party, until the day of the election,
November 6, he remained quietly at home. The strong
men of his party were ardently and harmoniously at
work; the speeches of Sumner, Chase, Cassius M. Clay,
and other eminent orators reported in the newspapers
were read by Mr. Lincoln and Mary. All day long
visitors thronged the house or crowded Lincoln's office;
some of them were interested friends, others were
strangers impelled by mere curiosity. One day an old
woman who had known him in New Salem brought
him a pair of woolen socks. She said, "I spun the yarn
and knit them socks myself." Many other gifts of
wearing apparel were sent, some from distant parts of
the country, which amused Mr. Lincoln very much.
Laughing heartily, he said, "Well, wife, if nothing
else comes out of this scrape, we are going to have
some new clothes." Mary's relatives in Springfield
were deeply interested and came every day to report
any letters or news received by them bearing on the
campaign and to hear any important information re-

ceived by the Lincolns. The mails flooded Mr. Lincoln with newspapers, some of them marked for his especial perusal; his tables were stacked with letters, few of which he had time to open and answer. The campaign of 1860 was excitingly under way. Mary Lincoln had no misgivings. She encouraged and stimulated her husband when he became despondent and rejoiced whole-heartedly at any good news.

On election day, November 6, Springfield was wide awake before daylight, and as Mary at the head of her table poured the breakfast coffee for Mr. Lincoln, she said with a light little laugh, "It is well that the strain will soon be over, my hand is trembling so that I nearly spilled your coffee." She was rejoiced to see that her husband was as calm and cool as though this were a colorless day instead of a red-letter one in their lives. Mr. Lincoln, as usual, went to the room reserved for him at the State House about eight o'clock and his friends thronged about him all day. Mary at home was anxiously waiting for news though no returns were expected until after seven o'clock. As the telegrams announcing one Lincoln majority after another came in, there was more and more excitement and enthusiasm throughout the city.

Mr. Lincoln, who in the afternoon had gone to the hall where the ladies of Springfield had prepared re-

freshments for the Republican politicians, later with-
drew to a telegraph office where returns could be
received more quietly: he was now uneasy only about
the vote in Springfield. Before daylight the welcome
announcement came that he had a majority in his own
precinct; turning to his friends, he said cheerfully,
"I guess I'll go home now." Mary, who had not gone
to bed at all, met him at the door; the strain had been
too great for her nerves, and she threw herself into her
husband's arms in a passion of tears. "There, there,
little woman," said Lincoln, patting her shoulder, "I
thought you wanted me to be President." "I do,"
sobbed Mary, "and I am very happy—that is why I
am crying," she said smiling up through her tears.

Two weeks after the election Mrs. Lincoln spent
several days in Chicago with her husband, where he
was to meet Hannibal Hamlin, the Vice President
elect. There was a large reception at the Tremont
House and a line of visitors passed for two hours and
a half shaking hands with Mr. Lincoln, who stood with
Mrs. Lincoln and Mr. Hamlin at his right.

On Jan. 10, 1861, Mrs. Lincoln, accompanied by her
brother-in-law, Mr. C. M. Smith, and the Hon. Amos
Tuck of New Hampshire, went to New York to make
purchases for the White House. After spending a few

days in New York, they went to Cambridge, Massachusetts, to visit Mrs. Lincoln's son Robert.

A letter from this young man written to Mary in the preceding month will show how calmly and sensibly he conducted himself during this exciting period.

> "Phillips Exeter Academy.
> December 2, 1860.

"Dear Mother:

"You see I am back at Exeter and I feel very much at home. I am here with Dick McConkey. We have been in a constant round of dissipation since we came. On Thursday we were at dinner at Miss Gales, on Friday Mr. Tuck gave a large party which passed off very finely. Mr. Tuck thinks of going to Chicago in about three weeks and thence to St. Louis, so look out for him. To-night we are invited out to tea which will wind up our fun, as we have to commence study again tomorrow. We have only about six weeks more before going home. I see by the papers that you have been to Chicago. Aren't you beginning to get a little tired of this constant uproar? I have a couple of friends, who are going to the inauguration after vacation is over and I have invited them to stop at our house on their road. They are nice fellows and have been with me for the last year. You will remember that I wrote to father about a fellow who is boring me considerably. He capped the climax lately. There was a Republican levee and supper at Cambridge to which I was invited. I did not go for I anticipated what really happened. I was sitting in my room about 6:30 when two boys came in and handed me an admission ticket, on the back of which the fellow had written asking me to come over as they were calling for me. I wrote him a note excusing myself. He must be the biggest fool in the world not to know I did not want to go over, when if I did I would be expected to make a speech! Just phancy my phelinks mounted on the rostrum holding 'a vast sea of human faces, etc.' I stop overwhelmed.

Yours affectionately,
R. T. LINCOLN."

Returning to Springfield Mary prepared for the social events connected with the coming departure to the national capitol. In the accepted style of the society reporter, a Springfield correspondent of the *Missouri Democrat* writes, on February 6, 1861:

"The first levee given by the President elect took place last evening at his own residence in this City and it was a grand outpouring of citizens and strangers together with the members of the Legislature. Your humble servant was invited to attend. Mr. Lincoln threw open his house for a general reception of all the people who felt disposed to give him and his Lady a parting call. The levee lasted from seven until twelve o'clock in the evening, and the house was thronged by thousands up to the latest hour. Mr. Lincoln received the guests as they entered and were made known. They then passed on and were introduced to Mrs. Lincoln who stood near the center of the parlor and who I must say acquitted herself most gracefully and admirably. She was dressed plainly but richly. She wore a beautiful full trail, white moire-antique silk, with a small French lace collar. Her neck was ornamented with a string of pearls. Her head dress was a simple and delicate vine arranged with much taste. She displayed but little jewelry and this was well and appropriately adjusted. She is a lady of fine figure and accomplished address and is well calculated to grace and do honor at the White House. She was on this occasion accompanied by four of her sisters,— Mrs. W. S. Wallace, Mrs. C. M. Smith of Springfield, Mrs. Charles Kellogg of Cincinnati, and a Miss Todd of Kentucky. They all appeared to be extremely happy and I hope there will be nothing thrown in their way to hinder them from experiencing in full all the pleasures which they now anticipate in coming events. I thought, when looking upon the lovely group of the Todd family, how proud old Kentucky would have felt if she could have been present to witness the position in which her son and daughters were placed. (T. W.)"

For four anxious months after the election of November 6, Mary had seen, with a sinking heart, the Southern States, one by one, withdraw from the Union; there was no doubt in the minds of the large majority of the Southern people that they had a Constitutional right to secede from the Union. Many in the North held the same opinion and had wished to secede from the South on account of their abhorrence of slavery. On November 10 the United States senators from South

Carolina resigned their seats at Washington, a few weeks later their State seceded and under the Palmetto Flag formed an independent government.

The Stars and Stripes, however, still floated over Fort Sumter in Charleston harbor, garrisoned by Federal troops under command of Colonel Robert Anderson of Kentucky. In January, Mississippi, Florida, Alabama, Georgia, and Louisiana adopted ordinances of secession. Mary had two sisters living in Selma, Alabama—Martha Todd married to Mr. Clement White, and Elodie Todd married to Colonel N. H. R. Dawson—and three of her brothers were living in New Orleans. Living on a Louisiana plantation was her stepmother's brother James Humphreys, who had married a charming New Orleans woman of French extraction. Her beauty and grace were inherited by their two attractive daughters, who in girlhood had often visited at her father's home in Lexington.

So patriotic indignation at seeing these States go out of the Union was mingled with personal sadness over a separation in sympathy and opinion of dear relatives and friends. And all her thoughts were tinctured with a feeling of undefined fear. She dreaded—she knew not what. War was unthinkable, yet in February, when a General Confederate Convention was held in Montgomery, Alabama, Mary with her political acumen began to sense hostilities of some sort, seeing how promptly and intelligently the seceding States were forming the Southern Confederacy and how resolutely they were seizing forts and arsenals and making every preparation to defend the newly formed nation. "Oh, will it never stop?" cried Mary to her husband. "Will inauguration day never come?"

Buchanan, the President in power, seemed to be a passive onlooker. Mary had known, of course, that the South would be dissatisfied with a Republican President, but she was filled with dismay when a furious clamor rose in influential quarters of the North, an insistent demand that Mr. Lincoln should declare himself and promise some concession which would quiet the unrest of the South and stop secession.

The New York *Herald* declared Lincoln was a "sectional President whom the South had no part in electing. If he comes out and tells the people that he will govern the country according to the views of the majority and not to serve the purpose of the minority, all may yet be well. Mr. Lincoln must throw his pledges to the wind, let his own party go to perdition in its own way, and devote himself to the service of the whole country. It is Mr. Lincoln's bounden duty to come out now and declare his views." Many of the "Republican" newspapers were urging Mr. Lincoln to make some sort of compromise; the Unionists of the South were urging him to say plainly that the South would have nothing to fear from his election. Mr. Lincoln had already expressed himself repeatedly on all these questions, and now declared, "Self-respect demands of me and of the party which has elected me that when threatened I should be silent."

His old friend and fellow Congressman Alexander H. Stephens, of Georgia, now Vice President of the Southern Confederacy, at this time wrote him: "The country is certainly in great peril; and no man ever had heavier or graver responsibilities resting upon him than you have in the present momentous crisis."

Lincoln replied: "I fully appreciate the present peril the country is in and the weight of responsibility on me. Do the people of the South really entertain fears that a Republican administration would directly or indirectly interfere with the slaves or with them about the slaves? If they do I wish to assure you, as once a friend, and still, I hope, not an enemy, that there is no cause for such fears. The South would be in no more danger in this respect than it was in the days of Washington. I suppose, however, this does not meet the case. You think slavery is right and ought to be extended, while we think it is wrong and ought to be restricted.

That I suppose is the rub. It certainly is the only substantial difference between us."

There was to Mary one crumb of comfort in the fact
that Kentucky showed no sign of seceding. She and
Mr. Lincoln pored over the Lexington, Kentucky,
paper, for which they had subscribed every year since
Mary's marriage, for news of the political bias of the
State of their birth, of their relatives and friends.
There were so many Unionists in Kentucky that Mary
and Mr. Lincoln hoped the sentiment would spread.
Mary knew that her own people were in favor of gradual emancipation, not merely in theory, but carried out
in actual practice as already stated in the case of her
step-grandmother. She knew too how her own people
felt about the selling of slaves; in their opinion only
the direst poverty could justify this and even then the
stigma of disgrace would cling to the seller of a slave
though not to the buyer of one.

Not only did Mary read Kentucky papers, she
scanned the news of the whole country. The press both
North and South teemed with advice to the President
elect; with prophecies of evil times. Private mail was
overflowing with the same kind of advice, with con-
demnation of Mr. Lincoln, and even with threats of
his assassination. All this told fearfully on Mr. Lincoln and Mary. Superstition in the nature of both was

aroused by a vision Mr. Lincoln had when, wearied by a day of distraction, he threw himself down on a lounge in his room and saw in a swinging mirror over a bureau, the image of himself reflected with two faces, one much paler than the other. Mary, with wide eyes, the color drained out of her face, feared the vision might mean that Mr. Lincoln would be elected twice as President, but would not live to finish out his second term and he was so deeply impressed by this vision that he told the incident some years later to Noah Brooks, the author.

Mr. Lincoln was feeling the terrible responsibility and difficulties of his situation and yet was forced to a policy of inaction, until after the inauguration. He was often filled with gloom and despondency which it took all of Mary's adroitness to dispel; he declared that he would willingly take out of his life "a period of years equal to the two months which intervenes between now and my inauguration, to take the oath of office now," because every hour was adding to his difficulties, and the outlook each day grew more gloomy. Mary was alternately filled with elation over her husband's coming inauguration as President and with fear lest some assassin might make good his threat. She breathed a sigh of relief when at last, on Monday, February 11, at eight o'clock in the morning the Presidential party was starting for Washington. All was bustle and excitement, but as Mr. Lincoln from the car platform made his farewell speech to the sea of friendly faces come to wish them Godspeed, a wave of sadness passed over Mary; she was leaving for years, perhaps forever, her home made dear by the one and great love of her life; the little grave of her baby; old and faithful friends—for a life new and untried, full of glorious possibilities, it is true, but of great uncertainty, and emotion gripped her throat and fear clutched her heart as she heard her husband say with a trembling voice, "Here my children have been born and one is buried. I now leave not knowing when or whether ever I may return."

Eight o'clock in the morning being an inconvenient hour, Mrs. Lincoln had decided to take a later train and join the Presidential party at Indianapolis, where they were to stay all night. As the special train conveying the President elect pulled out of Springfield, Mary Lincoln was standing on the platform, in the midst of their friends, waving him a farewell.

Accompanying Mary Lincoln from Springfield, to be present at the inauguration and to be her guests at the White House, were her sister Mrs. Ninian Edwards (Elizabeth Todd) with her two daughters, Mrs. Baker and Miss Edwards, and the daughter of her Uncle John, Mrs. Grimsley (Elizabeth Todd). Mrs. Edwards was a woman of great poise and dignity and a real help in any social dilemma; she had started her social career very early at the governor's mansion in Illinois when she was a young bride still in her teens. At Indianapolis, Mary, somewhat dazed, had to summon up her social resources for the public ordeal which awaited her, and which was to be repeated in other cities.

A huge public reception in the evening, elaborate in its preparations, a breakfast next morning with the governor of the State, and a reception at the hotel. At ten o'clock Tuesday morning Mr. Lincoln's party left Indianapolis for Cincinnati. "The train under way, all grew composed and even merry as the enthusiasm all along the line cheered them. Mary forgot her fear in her pride of her great husband. Everybody wanted to shake hands with him. Democrats as well as Republicans called out, "Good-bye, Abe, stick to the Constitution and we will stick to you."

Mary had recovered her spirits fully by this time. The towns through which they passed were decorated with flags, cheering men were eager to see Mr. Lincoln. A magnificent reception was given him in Cincinnati, and Mary with a little pressure on his arm reminded him that it was his birthday, which she and Mr. Lincoln, just the two of them, could celebrate with nods and shy coquettish glances from under Mary's long lashes, replied to by his grave and tender regard. They both thought of the modest little dinners of other birthdays on the 12th of February when they were at home with a few chosen and congenial friends come to wish Mr. Lincoln many happy returns, and when she would repeat the little speech she had made on his first birthday after their marriage which ended: "I am so glad you have a birthday. I feel so grateful to your mother."

Mr. Lincoln made two brief speeches in Cincinnati; he said that he had made but one speech before in that city and then much of what he said had been addressed to the Kentuckians. "Fellow citizens of Kentucky! friends! brethren! may I call you in my new position? I see no occasion, and feel no inclination, to retract a word of this. If it shall not be made good, be assured the fault shall not be mine."

Mr. Lincoln and Mary had a tender feeling for the State of their birth. Mr. Lincoln's three law partners were all born in Kentucky.

After leaving Cincinnati for Columbus on Wednesday morning, few stops were made. Another brilliant reception at Columbus, and on Thursday morning, February 14, the Presidential party was again on its way, and Lincoln that night spoke to an immense crowd at Pittsburgh. It is refreshing to note that the

HON. JOHN TODD STUART, MARY TODD'S COUSIN AND ABRAHAM LINCOLN'S
FIRST LAW PARTNER

MRS. JOHN TODD STUART

Pennsylvanians were not alarmed over the threatened dissolution of the Union but demanded a speech on the tariff.

At Cleveland, Buffalo, Albany, New York, crowds of cheering people, flowers, receptions, dinners, luncheons, flags floating, cannon booming. The journey through the State of New York occupied three days. Mary was in high spirits all the way. She remained with a party of eighteen or twenty relatives and friends in New York.

On February 23, at six o'clock in the morning, Mr. Lincoln was in Washington, safe in spite of rumors of plots to abduct him and threats of assassination. While his friends took these threats seriously, Mr. Lincoln was inclined to think their fears groundless. Rooms had been reserved for the Presidential party at Willard's Hotel. Mrs. Lincoln and her party were still in New York at the comfortable old Metropolitan Hotel and did not join Mr. Lincoln until the evening of March 2. From Saturday evening until Monday morning, the day of the inauguration, Mary Lincoln could not shake off a feeling of apprehension. If she forgot her fear for a moment, the soldiers thronging the streets and the guards stationed to protect her husband would remind her that her loved one was not yet out of danger; but, she would argue to herself, what ill could happen to him surrounded by all these loyal men, under all this watchful care? At that consoling thought her buoyant nature would reassert itself.

Senator James Harlan, of Mt. Pleasant, Iowa, met Mr. Lincoln for the first time a few days before the inauguration, and this meeting developed later into a warm friendship between the two families. He describes his impressions of the Lincolns thus:

"Abraham Lincoln was an unusually tall man, though he did not seem slender. He appeared to be as lean and his muscles as hard as those of a prize-fighter. He was obviously a very strong, powerful man, physically capable of immense endurance. His eyes slightly receded, were about normal in size and, according to my recollection gray in color—with no marked expression, except pensiveness and truthfulness. His head was large, both longitudinally and perpendicularly, with a tall and ample forehead. His hair was dark brown, without any tendency to baldness. His head, when he was in repose, drooped slightly forward, and his whole countenance was pensive to sadness. In conversation it would kindle into brightness; and with increased earnestness become luminous. He impressed everyone with his frankness and manifest candor, and conscious manly strength, free from the slightest manifestation of egotism. No one could look at him and doubt his perfect honesty, sincerity, and kindness.

"As I have sometimes heretofore said, and continue to think, no one can know a married man thoroughly, who does not also know his wife. I must add a few descriptive words of Mrs. Mary Todd Lincoln, wife of Abraham Lincoln.

"She was fair, of about medium height, but standing near her husband, by comparison seemed short. Her quiet, gentle manners and firm womanly bearing impressed everyone with the conviction that she was a well-educated, cultured lady, accustomed to the usages of society and with ability to take care of herself. She was a Kentuckian.

"Mr. and Mrs. Lincoln were, at that date, the parents of three living children about whom, perhaps, I ought to say a word or two; because the children brought up in a family usually reflect, like a mirror, the character of their parents.

"The oldest, Robert Todd Lincoln, was a youth of seventeen or eighteen years;—well developed physically, a strong, healthy, resolute, sensible-looking fellow; without the slightest appearance of ostentation or family pride on account of his father's election to the Presidency.

"The second child, William Lincoln, was probably

about twelve years of age. He was a beautiful boy; intelligent, polite, observant, careful of the comfort of others and courtly in his manners; so much so as to attract the attention and affection of everybody with whom he came in contact.

"The third child, Thomas Lincoln—usually called "Tad"—was a small boy, probably not more than seven or eight years old. He was apparently under little restraint, overflowing with the joys of his young life and almost constantly near and clinging to his father who never appeared to be annoyed by his freaks and capers."

On the 4th of March, Washington was stirring at the break of day. Mary Lincoln, sleepless and excited, saw from her window scores of people, who had been unable to find beds the night before on account of the crowded condition of hotels and boarding-houses, restlessly walking the streets; incoming trains were bringing fresh crowds to see the inauguration of the first Republican President; the tramp, tramp of soldiers, the rumble and clatter and clash of artillery, the shrill screams of newsboys all added to the general noise and confusion. Mr. Lincoln, at his rooms at Willard's Hotel, had from a very early hour been at work. At noon Mr. Buchanan, the President of the United States, came to escort the President elect to the

Capitol. They passed through lines of guards, platoons of soldiers, cavalry, infantry, artillery, for General Winfield Scott was determined that no harm should befall the incoming President.

Mrs. Lincoln and her party occupied the diplomatic gallery. Mary Lincoln had no eyes for the brilliant scene: the diplomatic corps glittering with decorations, the women in their beautiful gowns, had at this time no interest for her; with her soul in her eyes she saw only one loved face that meant home and all that was dear to her in the world. After the oath of office had been administered to Vice President elect Hannibal Hamlin, who made a short speech, there was a concerted movement in the direction of the east portico where a wooden platform had been erected for this occasion. The procession was headed by the Justices of the Supreme Court in their caps and silk gowns. Upon the front of the platform were the Senate Committee, President Buchanan, Chief Justice Taney and Mr. Lincoln; just back were seated Mrs. Lincoln, her three sons, Mrs. Grimsley and other relatives; the rest of the platform was filled with judges, senators, and other distinguished guests.

As Mr. Lincoln came to a table containing a Bible, a pitcher and a glass of water, he placed a manuscript on the table and his cane upon it as a paper weight;

lifting his hat he looked around for a place to put it when a hand reached over and took the hat, and Judge Stephen A. Douglas whispered to Mrs. Grimsley, "If I cannot be President, I can at least be his hat bearer." Mary Lincoln's heart warmed to the friend of her girl-hood as she saw this graceful act of courtesy. She saw her husband, tall, dignified, unexcited, very grave. His self-possession was perfect. His resonant voice, a little high-pitched, reached the outer fringes of the vast crowd in front of him. Mary listened dreamily to the Inaugural Address, which Mr. Lincoln had read to her the day before and which he was now delivering with as much ease as if such an address were an everyday occurrence.

Mary tried to realize that she and her husband had reached the crowning point of their ambition—would it mean joy or sorrow? Would they have to see the bitter animosities of North and South culminate in war or—— She started from her reverie to nod a hopeful assent to the closing sentences of the address: "I am loath to close. We are not enemies but friends." (And dear kindred, thought Mary.) "We must not be ene-mies. Though passion may have strained, it must not break our bonds of affection. The mystic chords of memory, stretching from every battlefield and patriot grave to every living heart and hearthstone all over this broad land will yet swell the chorus of the Union when again touched, as surely they will be, by the better angels of our nature." The oath prescribed by the Constitution was administered by Chief Justice Taney, and Abraham Lincoln was President of the United States.

Mary had a feeling of intense relief when, the ceremonies over and unmarred by any unfriendly demonstration, her husband was safe in what was to be their home, God willing, for the next four years. At the entrance of the executive mansion, "Old Edwards," the doorkeeper through many administrations, ushered them into a mansion swept and garnished, to be sure, but looking dull and shabby with its old and worn furnishings. The East, the Blue and the Red rooms were not quite so dingy, as all the elegance of the mansion seemed concentrated in these three rooms; now, however, there was too much excitement for Mary to have more than a fleeting thought that just as soon as possible she must brighten all this dinginess.

After a gay company of seventeen or eighteen people had finished dinner, all separated to rest and prepare for the Grand Inaugural Ball, which would usher in the first Republican President (and many people thought the last one). Mary Lincoln, whose task it would be to uphold the social end of the administration, assumed her new position with self-confidence and poise and, socially, a joyous fearlessness, meeting the public with unaffected cordiality. With a direct and searching glance, she could distinguish between enemies and friends. At first she was undismayed by the number of hostile critics, hoping, no doubt, by her own friendly attitude to disarm them; but as the weeks went by she felt the enmity was deeper than personality or any amount of friendliness could dissipate, and a woman even less high-spirited and sensitive than Mary Todd Lincoln would have been irritated by the attitude of some of the erstwhile leaders of society at the Capitol.

Southern women, especially those from Virginia and Maryland, boasting long lines of distinguished ancestry, had for many years held sway as social leaders in Washington. They represented a clique of wealth and social prestige, of refinement and good breeding, and had Mary Lincoln been the wife of a Southern or Democratic President, she would have had no difficulty in being recognized as one of them and easily could have become socially popular as First Lady. But President Lincoln as leader of the Republican party had aroused bitter resentment in the hearts of the Southern people; they declared he was an odious, tyrannical monster and his wife a renegade Southerner with no heart and no principles, they would have nothing to do with such a traitor! Southerners had no wish to overcome their prejudice against the wife of an Abolitionist, a word abhorrent to the South and, indeed, to a large faction in the North and East.

Leslie Perry some years since said in an article written for *Harper's Magazine:* "Every ingenuity of malice was resorted to to discredit the new régime. Both the President and his wife were mercilessly lampooned, and yet Mrs. Lincoln was the peer of any woman in Washington in education and character, as well as the 'barren ideality' of birth." And W. O. Stoddard declares she was bright, cheerful, almost merry sometimes—"as you look at her and talk with her the fact that she has so many enemies strikes you as one of the moral curiosities of this venomous time."

Whether through some misunderstanding or by order of General Beauregard, the Confederates fired on Fort Sumter on April 12, 1861, and the war between the North and South was on in deadly earnest. As Washington received the news of other States seceding, of riots and bloodshed in Baltimore, of bridges burned and railway communication with the North being cut off, the gloom and apprehension increased. Public buildings were barricaded, guards were camped in the East room and corridors of the White House. General

Cassius M. Clay (of Kentucky) with his Home Battalion was stationed in Willard's Hall. Patriotic fervor for the Union was intensified in the North, and higher and higher flamed the spirit of undying allegiance to the new-born league of independent States, the Southern Confederacy. For years the North and South had been stinging each other into uncontrollable madness. The North was singing, "We'll hang Jeff Davis on a Sour Apple Tree," and the South was substituting the name of Lincoln in the same song.

When a Southern girl in Washington at that hate-filled time saw Mrs. Lincoln's carriage approaching, she would run to the piano, fling wide the windows and sing "Dixie," "Maryland, My Maryland," or "Bonnie Blue Flag," and Mary's eyes would fill with tears for she knew this was done to hurt her. Neither did she fare better at the hands of the Northerners; she was accused, on account of her Southern birth, of being a Rebel at heart, of not sympathizing with her husband's views and principles. She was watched and spied upon for some clue upon which to hang a suspicion of her treachery to the Union—an unguarded word would have meant a volume of abuse or slander. With rare tact, following her husband's policy of conciliation, she tried to make friends of the opposition. In this social chaos and disruption she naturally turned first, for support, to women from her own State; among others, Mrs. John J. Crittenden, a handsome matron whose husband had left the Senate to become a representative and as such was the mover of the Crittenden Compromises calculated to restore the South to the Union by peaceful measures.

Also the wife of her old friend Stephen A. Douglas, the Democratic leader, was frequently asked to receive with Mrs. Lincoln. Mrs. Douglas, who combined wit and beauty with sweet gentle manners, was one of the belles of the White House. That Mrs. Lincoln should select for her receiving line the wives and daughters of Democrats gave great offense to many Republican women. Into this chaos of jealousies, animosities, private and public rancors, it would have been impossible to inject any of the beautiful quiet amenities of normal society. Ignoring this unpleasantness as much as possible, Mary Lincoln took her place as First Lady with simple, easy grace and dignity. She was sought by people of intellect who were charmed by her animation and originality of thought and her fearlessness in expressing herself. She was still strikingly youthful and attractive in appearance; she was "fair and forty," but not fat, as she weighed only a hundred and thirty pounds. Her hair, a lovely light chestnut with glints of bronze, had as yet not a gray thread. Her eyes sparkled youthfully with the zest of living, and the fashion of the day favored her mightily as her beautiful shoulders and arms gleamed like pearls in her low-cut short-sleeved evening gowns. She had individuality and distinction and an intellect and personality that caused her to be here admired, there envied, loved greatly by her friends, and deeply disliked by many outside her circle.

Her enthusiasms were so inspiring that a forlorn hope revived and blossomed in the down-hearted. Hence, her husband and friends brought to her many troubles and problems. She held her head high, slightly tilted back, possibly because she had so tall a husband to look up to. She was not tall, but seemed shorter than she really was by the side of her towering husband. More than merely pretty, she was both brilliant and fascinating, but, already prejudiced, nothing could mollify her critics. As they could not find any glaring faults in her behavior, they criticized her extravagance in dress.

Mary Lincoln, full of ardor and patriotism, wished to join a society pledged to use no foreign dress goods, laces or jewels during the war. But this project was condemned by Mr. Lincoln and Salmon P. Chase, his Secretary of the Treasury, who declared the Government needed the revenue coming from the importation of these luxuries. This made the wearing of rich clothing no crime, but rather a patriotic duty for all who could afford it. Mary Lincoln, with a keen appreciation of all that was exquisite and beautiful and with an instinctive talent for style and dress, became noted for elegant and costly apparel. She had very little lace, but that was of the finest rose point, Honiton or English thread; and her jewels, while not magnificent and consisting mostly of small pearls finely strung in dainty design and small diamonds set down closely in pearls (pavé, I think the French call it), were unusual and especially appealing to a refined and cultured taste.

President Lincoln loved to see Mary "dressed up"; he noticed her "fine feathers" and never failed to compliment her when she, with guileless vanity, pirouetted around the room for him to admire some particularly pretty dress, and he, smiling, would comment, "Our cat has a long tail to-night" or "Some of that tail might be added to the top."

With her husband's praises ringing in her ears, little did Mary Lincoln dream that her innocent love for beautiful clothes would one day cause her the deepest humiliation.

The bombardment of Fort Sumter by the Confederates, April 12, sounded the death knell of peace between the North and South. A few days later Virginia was open to Confederate troops, and from the White House windows the occupants looked upon green bluffs across the Potomac belonging to the enemy.

The death, Friday morning, May 23, of the dashing, gallant young Colonel Ellsworth, brought the first sting of sorrow to the White House. Colonel Ellsworth had come from Springfield with the Presidential party and was a member of the President's household. Colonel Ellsworth saw the President with a face of gloom, time and again, standing before the south windows of the White House looking through his glass at a Confederate flag flying from a staff at Alexandria. When the advance was made across the river to seize the heights from Arlington to Alexandria, Colonel Ellsworth, who had organized the New York Zouaves, took command and in hauling down this flag from the roof of a hotel, the owner and proprietor of the house killed him and was in turn immediately shot to death by one of Ellsworth's men. President and Mrs. Lincoln felt his loss keenly. The funeral services were held in the East room of the executive mansion, and the President and Mrs. Lincoln were in the line of carriages which conveyed the young soldier to the railway

station. The next death to make a gap in the ranks of
their friends was Stephen A. Douglas, June 3, 1861, for
in spite of political differences the close association of
their early life with the "Little Giant," his many generous impulses and very agreeable and lovable personality made a kindly bond, and the breaking of it was
painful to them both.

Early in the morning July 21, Washington was filled
with excitement. The booming of cannon at Bull Run
could be distinctly heard, and news at first was hopeful
for the Unionists. Soon, however, joy was turned to
consternation and panic when a telegram announced,
"The day is lost, save Washington and the remnant of
the Army." The family at the White House, feverishly anxious all day, saw daylight fade into night and
still had no thought of sleep when General Scott at two
A. M. came to bring tidings of relief. General Scott
insisted that Mrs. Lincoln and the boys should be sent
North out of danger. Mrs. Lincoln turned to her husband and, knowing full well what his answer would be,
asked, "Will you go with us?" "Most assuredly I will
not leave at this juncture," he answered promptly.
Just as promptly came the response from Mary Lincoln, "Then I will not leave you at this juncture."

Made brave by her devotion to her husband, the little
wife only thought of how she might shield or protect

him or at least share the danger with him. No urging moved her from this firm determination.

There was not much time in those fearful days for Mary Lincoln to give serious thought to the social disaffection. It was annoying, of course, and an added burden, but, surrounded by love as she was, it did not affect her happiness. Her two boys, Willie and Tad, were lively youngsters. Tad had much of his mother's mercurial disposition and the White House echoed with his laughter all day. The two boys were full of life and fun and their pranks, which sometimes called for chiding from their mother, gave great delight and amusement to their father. Willie was tall for eleven years of age, handsome, studious, remarkably intelligent, he was the pride and joy of his mother and father. Robert, who developed into the distinguished man known on both sides of the Atlantic, was at college and only occasionally at Washington.

Mrs. Grimsley, who had been Mrs. Lincoln's intimate girlhood friend and her bridesmaid, was at the White House with her for six months. The White House was always filled with friends and relatives of President and Mrs. Lincoln who were warmly hospitable. Mrs. Lincoln's two half-sisters, Mrs. Charles Kellogg (Margaret Todd) of Cincinnati and Mrs. Clement White (Martha Todd) of Selma, Alabama,

MARY TODD AT THE TIME LINCOLN MET HER
Painted by Katherine Helm from a daguerreotype

ABRAHAM LINCOLN AS HE APPEARED WHEN MARY TODD FIRST MET HIM
From a daguerreotype made about 1887 owned by the Lincoln family

had come on to be present at the inaugural ceremonies. Mrs. White was accused of smuggling quinine through the lines for sick Southern soldiers, but except for a small one-ounce package for her own use she was guiltless of this charge.

The true story is this: "Mattie" Todd was a brilliant young woman, more than usually attractive, and in appearance, mind, and manner more like Mary Lincoln than any of her sisters. She was a great favorite with her brother-in-law. Her visits to Washington were frequent and as President Lincoln did not wish the war to interrupt them he gave her a pass which would admit her through the lines at any point she chose. On one of these visits, not wishing to burden the White House with two trunks, she had left a "Saratoga," which the great unwieldy things were called, in care of two Baltimore friends at a hotel in Washington. The trunk contained wearing apparel which she would not need during her short visit at the White House. Handing the key to one of her friends, she said, "I do not think I will need it, but if I send a messenger, please go into the trunk and send me a blue brocade gown, which you will find in the top tray."

When Mrs. White called at the hotel for her trunk at the expiration of her visit to the White House, her friends had returned to Baltimore leaving the key of

her trunk at the hotel office. An officer who had followed Mrs. White insisted on examining her baggage.
Mrs. White was very indignant, showed the inspector
her pass and declared that she had nothing contraband.
The inspector touched his cap and left without further
molesting her. What was her amazement and morti-
fication on opening her trunks later to find a splendid
sword and a uniform for General Robert E. Lee, which
her Baltimore friends, without asking her permission
and without her knowledge, had stored in her trunk.
Her first impulse was to return immediately to the
White House and explain the whole matter to President Lincoln; her second thought was a fear that she
might imperil her friends who often visited Washington. She decided she had better seek wise council in
this dilemma.

On her arrival at Richmond, Virginia, she at once
consulted President Davis, whom she knew as well as
she did her brother-in-law—should she carry the sword
and uniform back to Washington and deliver them to
President Lincoln? Of course, he need never know,
but she would feel dishonest not to tell him about it.
President Davis decided that General Lee should have
the sword and the uniform, but Mrs. White was so
mortified and worried over the matter, that President
Davis, who had for many years been on pleasant terms

with Mrs. White's brother-in-law, wrote a personal letter, with his own hand, to President Lincoln explaining the position of Mrs. White. Mrs. White went with this letter to Washington, and the Great Man at the White House took the incident good-naturedly, twitting Mattie about her indignant lie to the inspector. This was the last time Mrs. White ever saw her brother-in-law or her sister Mary. She and her husband were going immediately south, for their hearts were with the Confederacy. This contretemps was always a source of regret to Mrs. White, who was entirely innocent of any complicity in passing contraband articles through the lines.

The other sister, Mrs. Charles Kellogg, who had come to see the inaugural ceremonies, was on her way with her husband to spend several years in Europe. Most of the time they were in Italy with Mr. Minor Kellogg (a brother of Charles Kellogg), who was an artist and made his home in Rome.

About the middle of April, 1861, Ben Hardin Helm went to Washington in response to a cordial personal letter of invitation from his brother-in-law, President Lincoln. Although Lincoln knew that Helm was a strong Southern-rights Democrat, on the 27th of April he handed him a sealed envelope. "Ben," he said, "here is something for you. Think it over by yourself and let

me know what you will do." The envelope contained
a commission as paymaster in the United States Army
with rank of major. This was the opportunity of
Helm's life. He knew the position was one of the most
coveted in the service. The rank of major at his age,
thirty, was very exceptional in the army. Nothing had
ever touched Helm like this.

"The position you offer me is beyond what I had
expected in my most hopeful dreams. It is the place
above all others which suits me, Lincoln," said Helm.
"You have been kind and generous to me beyond anything I have known. I have no claim upon you, for I
opposed your candidacy and did what I could for the
election of another, but with no unkindly feeling towards you; I wish I could see my way. I will try to
do what is right. Don't let this offer be made public
yet. You shall have my answer in a few days."

Helm had graduated from West Point in the class of
1851, but on account of ill health had been compelled
to resign from the service. In common, however, with
all the graduates of the military academy, he longed to
get back into the military service and this was a brilliant opportunity. He saw many of his old army com-
rades and had a talk that same afternoon with Colonel
Robert E. Lee of the Second Cavalry.

Helm, seeing that Colonel Lee was laboring under

strong emotion of some kind, anxiously inquired, "Are you not well, Colonel Lee?"

"Well in body but not in mind," replied the stately soldier, who looked the gentleman of long lineage that he was. He added sadly, "I have just resigned my commission in the United States Army. In the prime of life I quit a service wherein were all my expectations and hopes in this world."

Helm handed Colonel Lee the letter from Mr. Lincoln offering Helm the position of major and paymaster with rank from that date. Colonel Lee read it without a word.

"Did you know Mr. Lincoln is my brother-in-law?" asked Helm.

"No, I did not," said Colonel Lee, "but now let me say one word. I have no doubt of his [Lincoln's] kindly intentions, but he cannot control the elements. There must be a great war. I cannot strike at my own people, so to-day I wrote out my resignation and have asked General Scott as a favor for its immediate acceptance. My mind is too much disturbed to give you any advice. But do what your conscience and honor bid."

Neither did Helm doubt the good intentions of Mr. Lincoln, he knew his brother-in-law's kindly feelings towards the South. But could one man stem the tide of bitterness and hatred that was forcing the two sections into mortal conflict? Helm's father, Governor Helm, although a large slave owner, was a strong Union man at the beginning of the war. Kentucky had declared for neither side though the sentiment was strongly Southern, to use a slang expression, current at that time, "she was on the fence" and "she sat on the fence cheering both sides enduring of the war, though she pretty nigh fell off on the South side," as an old soldier said after hostilities were over. He did not quite know whether to be proud of her for this indecision. Mary Lincoln was hoping to have her beautiful young sister Emilie (Helm's wife) in Washington with her. "Emilie will be a belle at the White House receptions and we will be so proud of her," smiled Mary, and "we need scholarly dignified young men like yourself to ornament our army."

"The ideal career was before me," said General Helm. "The highest positions in the profession for which I was educated were opened to me in one day. I would not only be the youngest officer of my rank in the army, but could have transferred at the earliest possible moment to one of the cavalry regiments. With the changes occurring in them by resignation, I would certainly have been a full colonel within the year." Helm realized the possibilities open to him, that he would have a brilliant career in the profession for which he was eminently fitted. Added to this he had a sincere love for Mary Lincoln and the President, their attitude towards him was most affectionate and their estimate of his ability was extremely gratifying to Helm. "Good-bye" said Mary, sending a kiss for Emilie. "We hope very soon to see you both in Washington." And with a warm clasp of the hand for Lincoln, Helm and his brother-in-law parted never to meet again in this life. When Helm returned to Kentucky he met in Frankfort General Simon Bolivar Buckner, who had been his instructor at West Point and for whom he had a warm friendship, and his friend, Tom Monroe, then Secretary of State, an impassioned States' Rights man. Helm talked with many of his friends, most of whom were going South.

General Buckner had been made inspector-general of Kentucky, with rank of major-general. Kentucky was in a furore of excitement. Helm could not remain in this fierce contest unmoved and, like Colonel Lee, he felt that he could not strike against his own people. He wrote to President Lincoln, declining the position of paymaster. In the War Department is this record: Helm, Ben Hardin, nominated for paymaster in the United States Army, April 27, 1861. Declined."

"I had a bitter struggle with myself," said General

Helm; "such an opportunity rarely offers itself in a
lifetime. The most painful moment of my life was
when I declined the generous offer of my brother-in-
law." At least twice in 1861 and 1862 did General
Helm find opportunity to send kindly messages to
President Lincoln. He believed in Lincoln's sincerity,
and a difference in views could not affect his love for
Mary and his brother-in-law.

Among the friends and relatives from Springfield
who were frequent guests at the White House were
Mrs. Lincoln's cousins, John T. Stuart and Stephen
T. Logan, also Mrs. Lincoln's nieces, and her sister
Mrs. Ninian Edwards.

Living in Washington at that time were some kins-
men of Mary Lincoln's stepmother. John C. Breckinridge, United States Senator from Kentucky, who
later was a major-general in the Confederate Army.
Tall, dignified, and strikingly handsome, he com-
manded attention in any assembly of men. Governor
Gratz Brown of Missouri, Postmaster-General Montgomery Blair, and General Frank P. Blair; the latter
having married his cousin, Miss Appelline Alexander
of Versailles, Kentucky, also a kinswoman of Mrs.
Todd, made in that case a still closer tie. On the
strength of these family connections, Mary was hailed
by them as "Cousin Mary" and, according to the good

old clannish Kentucky custom of claiming relationship as far off as possible, they evidently extended this cousinly regard to Mary's cousins, for Mrs. Grimsley writes:

"My relation on the other side of the house, General John C. Breckinridge, was open and above board. He called a number of times, before leaving Washington, and most complacently said to me, 'Cousin Lizzie, I would not like you to be disappointed in your expected stay at the White House, so I will now invite you to remain here as a guest, when the Confederation takes possession.' Mrs. Lincoln replied, 'We will only be too happy to entertain her until that time, general.' Whereupon arose a seemingly merry war of words, but there was a perceptible undercurrent of storm and sting, as would naturally be the case when two bright, quick, embittered brains and tongues wage a contest. And this was not an unequal one, for Mrs. Lincoln was a woman of fine native mental qualities, vivacious, intellectual, and a charming conversationalist."

Mrs. Lincoln wrote that Senator Harris came frequently to the drawing room at the White House and, finding Senator Sumner there, said in his cheerful way, "Ah, Sumner, we are sure of finding you here." And Senator Sumner replied, "This is the first administration in which I have ever felt disposed to visit the house, and I consider it a privilege."

Senator Sumner "was a model of forensic elegance, scholarly culture, and precision." He spoke even in ordinary conversation with great care and fastidiousness in the choice of words. He was equally fastidious in his style of dress and was easily the Beau Brummell of the Senate. His wide reading and anti-slavery views made him very congenial to President and Mrs. Lincoln, who classed him as one of their most valued friends—a friendship which was amply proven when he so valiantly battled for a pension for the widow of the slain President.

Washington being extremely trying during the summer months, it was decided that Mrs. Lincoln should get a breath of fresh air at Long Branch and Saratoga. There she nursed Tad through a spell of illness, and later had to send her regrets to a large ball given in her honor on account of the severe illness of her friend Mrs. Shearer.

On her return to Washington in November, Mrs. Lincoln found her husband weighed down with cares of state, looking thin, careworn, and anxious. The whole town was in a turmoil of excitement. Everybody was eager for the latest news from the seat of war. There were groans of sorrow and shouts of joy.

The White House was thronged from morning until night with office-seekers, pardon-seekers, and sight-seeing strangers. No rest, no peace, her beloved husband looking more pitifully careworn and sad each day.

At the battle of Ball's Bluff, October 21, in the death of Colonel E. D. Baker (for whom they had named their second son), President and Mrs. Lincoln lost one of their oldest and dearest friends. Not only did they grieve sincerely, but the children, Willie and Tad, who loved him, could not be consoled, Willie wrote the following verses which appeared in the *National Republican:*

"Washington, D. C.
October 30, 1861.

Dear Sir:

I enclose you my first attempt at poetry.

Yours truly,

WM. W. LINCOLN."

To the Editor of the *National Republican Times.*

On the Death of Colonel Edward Baker

There was no patriot like Baker
So noble and so true;
He fell as a soldier on the field
His face to the sky of blue.

His voice is silent in the hall
Which oft his presence graced,

No more he'll hear the loud acclaim
Which rang from place to place.

No squeamish notions filled his breast
The Union was his theme.
No surrender and no compromise
His day thought and nights dream.

His country has her part to pay
To'rds those he left behind
His widow and his children all
We must always keep in mind.

CHAPTER IX

SHADOWS

AT NO time in the history of our country was any President's wife ever placed in such a trying position as fell to the lot of Mary Lincoln. President Lincoln was lovingly called the "Great Emancipator" by one section; "The Abolitionist" with unmitigated scorn by the other. Mrs. Lincoln, in company with her husband, was reviled by Southerners, contemptuously thought of as a traitor to her people and their principles. On the other hand, being Southern-born of a Southern-sympathizing family, with four brothers in the Confederate Army and three brothers-in-law officers in the same service and hosts of other friends and relatives in the south wearing "the gray," [1] the Northerners distrusted her, feared her, hated her, insulted her—all without cause, for she believed with all her soul in her husband's policies, and of the principles which he advocated she had been ardently in favor

---

[1] George Todd, surgeon in Confederate service, Mary Lincoln's full brother, survived the war many years; Samuel Todd, killed at Shiloh; David Todd, never recovered from wound received at Vicksburg. Though reported "dying," he survived, an invalid, for a few years after the war was over; Alexander Todd, killed at Baton Rouge; General Ben Hardin Helm, killed at Chickamauga (married Emilie Todd); Colonel N. H. R. Dawson, Selma, Alabama (married Elodie Todd); Captain Clem B. White (married Martha Todd).

since her girlhood. When she was about sixteen years old several occurrences besides the selling of old King Solomon, which incident, related in an earlier chapter, had roused her indignation, made her feel that the institution of slavery was wrong.

Mary had grown to young womanhood with the hope and belief that all slaves should and would be gradually emancipated, but she felt it only right that slaves should be taken care of by their owners until they reached an age where they could support themselves as directed by the will of Mrs. Humphreys. And now, in 1861, her vivid imagination pictured the negro free, civilized—she would talk by the hour of schemes for the betterment and the colonization of the negro; she would get quite breathless with interest and excitement. The negro would have little chance in a white man's country where equality, social and political, would always be denied him, but, led by a few superior and well-educated negroes like Fred Douglass, what might they not attain of greatness in their own native country! A vast country of undiscovered wealth, the white man would some day awake to its possibilities, and the negroes' toil would fill the white man's pocket. Why should not the negro benefit by the wealth of his own country produced by his own labor? He would thrive and grow fat in a climate which would spell death to a white man.

Mary Lincoln made at this time some very true and lasting friends. Those who knew her best were her greatest admirers. Mrs. Bates, whose husband was attorney-general in Lincoln's cabinet, expressed the warmest sympathy for Mrs. Lincoln, "whose trials were many and known to but few. As the wife of a man under constant hostile criticism, she received scant courtesy in some quarters. Mrs. Lincoln lived for her husband and children, banishing before a never flagging cheerfulness her husband's cares of office while at home."

Frank G. Carpenter, who lived at the White House for several months while painting the famous picture "Reading the Emancipation Proclamation," said of her: "She was a very brilliant woman, an excellent linguist, speaking French as easily as her native tongue. There is no denying a quality and quantity of high spiritedness in her temperament."

General Sickles, in an address, said: "It was my privilege to know President Lincoln and his consort through all the years they spent at the White House. I have never seen a more devoted couple. He always called her Mother and she always called him Father. In their domestic relations and in their devotion to their children, I have never seen a more congenial couple. He always looked to her for comfort and consolation in his troubles and cares. Indeed, the only joy poor Lincoln knew after reaching the White House were his wife and children. She shared all his troubles and never recovered from the culminating blow when he was assassinated."

John Lothrop Motley's account of an interview he had with her in the White House after his return from Europe, where he had met the most accomplished and elegant women in London and Vienna, is certainly worthy of consideration. Mr. James G. Blaine also spoke of her in terms of great admiration.

It had been decided that in these troublous times a seeming show of cheerfulness at the White House would put heart into the soldiers. There must be no indication of sadness at the Capitol to cast an additional gloom of uncertainty over the North, so the usual round of receptions, levees, and dinners for the winter season of 1862 were being planned. The first day of January was ushered in by President and Mrs. Lincoln with a New Year's reception. In February little Willie (William Wallace) became very ill, and his mother, frantic with anxiety, hung over him with loving care, oblivious of every other thing in the world. If she could only save the life of her little blue-eyed boy, nothing else mattered. The child's father, too, spent every minute he could spare from the duties of state, in the sickroom.

Here is a clipping from a Washington paper headed, "Sickness in the President's family."

"It was announced yesterday that the usual Saturday receptions at the White House and the levee on Tuesday would be omitted on account of the illness of the second son of the President, an interesting lad of about eight years of age, who has been lying dangerously ill of bilious fever for the last three days. Mrs. Lincoln has not left his bedside since Wednesday night, and fears are entertained for her health. This evening the fever has abated and hopes are entertained for the recovery of the little sufferer."

In spite, however, of every effort made to save him, Willie died on February 20, and the grief of his parents was too deep for them ever to allude to this sorrow.

Nathaniel Parker Willis pays Willie this tribute in the *Home Journal:* "This little fellow had his acquaintances among his father's friends, and I chanced to be one of them. He never failed to seek me out in the crowd, shake hands and make some pleasant remark; and this in a boy of ten years of age was, to say the least, endearing to a stranger. But he had more than mere affectionateness. His self-possession—

aplomb, as the French call it—was extraordinary. I
was one day passing the White House when he was
outside with a play-fellow on the side walk. Mr.
Seward drove in with Prince Napoleon and two of his
suite in the carriage, and in a mock-heroic way—terms
of amusing intimacy evidently existing between the
boy and the secretary—the official gentleman took off
his hat, and the Napoleon party did the same, all making the young prince President a ceremonious salute.
Not a bit staggered with the homage, Willie drew himself up to his full height, took off his little cap with
graceful self-possession, and bowed down formally to
the ground, like a little ambassador. They drove past
and he went on unconcerned with his play; the im-
promptu readiness and good judgment being clearly a
part of his nature. His genial and open expression of
countenance was none the less ingenuous and fearless
for a certain tincture of fun, and it was in this mingling
of qualities that he so faithfully resembled his father."

Mr. Lincoln tried in many ways to distract Mary's
mind from the grief which was consuming her.

Madame Patti being in Washington soon after
Willie's death, Mr. Lincoln invited her to the White
House. Mr. Lincoln had met Patti in concert with
Ole Bull in 1853 when Patti was only ten years of age;

and at that time, in speaking of her to Mary, had pre-
dicted for her a great future.   Patti says, (*Courier-
Journal,* Louisville, Kentucky) :

"The following afternoon my manager took me to
the White House and we were received by Mrs. Lincoln in one of the big parlors.   The President's wife
was a handsome woman, almost regal in her deep black
and expansive crinoline, only an outline of white at
throat and wrists.   Her manner was most gracious
without a particle of reserve or stiffness.   'My dear, it
is very kind of you to come to see us,' she said.   Taking both my hands in hers and smiling in my face, she
added, 'I have wanted to see you ;—to see the young girl
who has done so much, who has set the whole world
talking of her wonderful singing.'

"Then the President entered the room.   He greeted
us cordially, and again mentioned the great change in
me since the Ole Bull concert.   'I shall always regret,
Mary, that you were not with me at that time,' he said,
turning to his wife.   'I, too,' she replied, 'have regretted it.'   Without waiting to be asked, I volunteered
to sing for Mrs. Lincoln.   'Thank you so much, my
dear,' she said.   I drew off my gloves and went to the
piano.   Mr. Strakosch accompanied me in a couple of
rather florid things.   Then I sang to my own accom-

paniment, 'The Last Rose of Summer.' When I had finished the last long-drawn-out note of the song, I turned to have a look at my audience. Mrs. Lincoln had risen from her seat and was standing at a window in the back part of the room with her back toward me. I could not see her face but I knew she was weeping. The melancholy strains of the ballad had set her heart aching with renewed sadness. I felt I had made an awkward choice."

After singing, at Mr. Lincoln's request, "Home, Sweet Home," Patti was so wrought up over the situation that she says she was weeping herself as she took leave of the bereaved parents.

In addition to her grief over her little son's death, Mary Lincoln, loving her own family with warm-hearted clannishness, was filled with apprehension on their account. As one after another of her brothers fell in the Confederate service, her heart was torn with more and more sorrow.

When the Civil War broke out Mary Lincoln had five living brothers. Levi Todd (her full brother) was living in Lexington, Kentucky. He was a Unionist, but his health was too infirm for him to take an active part in the hostilities, and before the war came to an end he was buried from the home of his stepmother in

Lexington. Three of her brothers were living in New Orleans. Dr. George Todd (her full brother) was early appointed surgeon in the Confederate service and survived the war for many years. Sam and David Todd were in business in New Orleans, and Alexander, the youngest of the Todd brothers, who was living in Kentucky at the commencement of the war, became aide-de-camp to his brother-in-law General Ben Hardin Helm.

In March, 1862, when Beauregard was appointed to the West and sent out to stay the progress of the Federal Army under Grant and Sherman through Kentucky and Tennessee, he made a call upon Louisiana, his native State, to come to his aid. Among the several thousand young and ardent volunteers was young Sam Todd, who enrolled himself in Company I, Crescent Regiment. A month later he lost his life in the fierce battle of Shiloh.

The Richmond (Va.) *State* contained this article:

"The day before the battle of Shiloh was fought the writer and several others gave a dinner to some half a dozen of their personal friends of the Crescent Regiment, Washington Artillery, etc.; and Sam Todd was one of the favorite guests, jovial Sam Todd! Who that knew him can ever forget him—all soul—all fun and fire too—he was a

gay happy youth of splendid address and fine social position, handsome in person and very popular. Being an
ardent Southerner his standing among his friends was not
injured by his being a brother-in-law of the President or
'Old Abe' as Lincoln was called.

"The diners separated for the march and the next day
by sunrise were in the midst of battle. The first day,
though the battle was fierce, desperate and hotly contested
the Confederates were happy at scoring a victory. They
slept on the field in a drenching rain with logs for pillows.
In the morning they were all up and in line. Before advancing, while some one was boiling coffee and others were
boiling a pot of potatoes, a young fellow in the uniform
of the Crescents came up and expressed a wish for one of
the 'Murphys' when they were done. It was Sam Todd
who was congratulated on his good fortune in the fight—
before Sam got the 'Murphy' the order came to fall in at
once as the Federals were advancing in force. It was the
new troops of Buell and Nelson. Sam Todd's regiment
was promptly thrown to the front and Sam with a bullet
in his forehead was one of the first to fall. The Confederates were driven back and still further back, leaving
their dead on the field to be buried with grim and hasty
funeral rites by Grant. Among them there was no better
man or more devoted soldier of the Confederacy than this
gallant young brother of the 'Lady of the White House'."

The "Lady of the White House" received this news
with a heavy heart. Sam dead on the field of battle!

Sam, the baby brother she had loved to cuddle when old Mammy Sally had allowed her to hold him a few minutes when she was a little girl; the baby so tiny and fragile that she had confided to Mrs. Clay he was too soft to be healthy. Sam, who was so handsome, so courtly.

When she last saw him in Kentucky, the Todds were all out in the country at Buena Vista. They were saddened then at the loss of her father and little Eddie, but happy in contrast with the grief-stricken present. How well Sam looked on horseback—how she had enjoyed riding with him—and Mary Lincoln, with purple rings under her dry eyes, bit her trembling lips to hold back her heavy sobs. She must not betray her grief. In helping others perhaps she might find comfort, so much of her time was given to visiting hospitals. Some presents of wine came to the White House about this time, champagne, green seal and other seal, white wine from the Rhine, wines from Spain and Portugal, brandy, Jamaica rum. "They do not seem to have forgotten anything," said Mrs. Lincoln. "But what shall I do with it? Mr. Lincoln never touches any strong drink. I never use it. I will thank these gentlemen, and the poor sick soldiers shall have it all." She was exceedingly pleased to have such a carefully selected medical supply to distribute.

"Executive Mansion, Washington
August 16, 1862.

"Hon. Hiram Barney
New York.

Mrs. L. has $1000 for the benefit of the hospitals, and she will be obliged and send the pay if you will be so good as to select and send her $200 worth of good lemons and $100 worth of good oranges.

A. LINCOLN."

The *Chronicle,* November 29, 1862:

"Mrs. Lincoln returned to Washington on Thursday evening, apparently much improved by her visit to the North. The sick and wounded soldiers in our hospitals will hail her return with joy."

Mrs. Lincoln was seen many times a week at the hospitals, attendants carrying baskets of dainties especially prepared at the White House and baskets of flowers to cheer the sick soldiers. A letter written by an old soldier when he heard of Mrs. Lincoln's death will show how welcome her visits were.

"The death of the widow of the great Emancipator will cause a feeling of sorrow all over this country but it will be a cause of particular sorrow to the soldiers of the Army of the Potomac who, sick or wounded in the Washington hospitals, were the objects of her especial care and attention. At the first battle of Fredericksburg I received a painful

wound in the face * * * among the many who came to the
hospital to speak cheering words to the afflicted none was
more kind or showed a nobler spirit than the wife of the
Chief Magistrate of the Nation. She called regularly,
bringing with her by attendants flowers, fruits and delicacies
and bestowing them with her own hand with a grace worthy
of the station she held * * * she lives in the memory of
those whose agonies she soothed with loving words.

FRANK G. THOMPSON."

Newspaper clipping, 1862—"Mrs. Lincoln":

"Now for our own country, with its ordeal of fire and
its baptism of blood. The lady who presides as the wife
of the Chief Magistrate brought with her from the West a
reputation for refinement and love of the beautiful that
has been admirably realized. The stamp of her exquisite
taste is left on the furnishing of the Presidential Mansion,
that never looked so well as now; and though in deepest
mourning there is a delicacy displayed in the arrangement
of her toilette that is unequaled in any country for its
classic adaptation and elegance. She possesses that calm
and conscious dignity, that is unruffled by envy and unsul-
lied by detraction, though malice hides itself in the tongues
of the Secessionists. She was celebrated for her conver-
sational powers in the society in which she moved in St.
Louis and at Chicago, and her kindness and cordiality has
acted like oil poured on troubled waters here. In youth
she must have been very beautiful and 'like light within a
vase' her whole features illuminate with their joyous sparkle

of a cultivated intellect. Well may Dr. Russell say 'I was never more disappointed [surprised?] in any person than Mrs. Lincoln; her manners would adorn a court.' The atmosphere of elevated sentiments, such as seeks companionship with the divine virtues of our nature and never descends from its higher sphere dwells and abides with her. Her voice is rich with the cadence of a pure and patriotic and womanly heart. In her mission of mercy to sick soldiers she fears no disease, and having felt deep bereavement herself, she gently dries the tears of the widow and the orphan. Such is she, to whom God grant many long and sunny days on earth to do his good word and work."

The second sad summer wore away. Hardly a day passed that Mary Lincoln's heart was not wrung with fear on account of letters warning the President of assassination. When she saw him preparing for a walk she would cling to him, and beg him not to leave the White House without a guard; when the President laughed at her fears and assured her that her imagination was playing her tricks, she would look up into his face with a brave little smile, but in her heart was fear. The strain of the war, her incurable grief for Willie, the suppressed anxiety for her Southern kindred, and this ever-clutching fear for her husband's safety were slowly, relentlessly, sapping her life and strength. At the least noise, the ringing of a bell, the dropping of a book, her face would be drained of color, and her hand would fly to her heart in sudden and uncontrollable panic. November brought the news that another brother, David Todd, lay mortally wounded after the battle of Vicksburg and his sister at the White House, with a frozen smile on her lips and a heart of lead, must listen to the shouts of rejoicing over Grant's victory. While her brother lay dying she must shed no tear, utter no word of grief lest it be construed as sympathy for the Southern cause. The President appreciated his wife's efforts at self-control and his love for her was very tender and protective.

> "Executive Mansion, Washington
> December 21, 1862.
>
> "Mrs. A. Lincoln
> Continental Hotel,
> Philadelphia.
>
> Do not come on the night train. It is too cold. Come in the morning.
>
> A. LINCOLN."

Christmas, 1862, Washington for the Federals was filled with gloom. The Confederates had been successful in the fighting around Fredericksburg, Virginia. Washington was filled with wounded and dying men, nevertheless, the administration demanded that the festivities of the holiday season must be observed. The gloom and discouragement must not be acknowledged. The President on New Year's morning at eleven o'clock received the shining officials of the diplomatic corps and the officers of the army and navy who happened to be in town. At twelve o'clock noon the gates of the White House grounds were flung wide, and the clamorous people were admitted in instalments.

The President and Mrs. Lincoln must wear smiling faces even if their eyes were far away with sad thoughts. And now that Robert was pleading to leave college and enter the army, a new anxiety was looming big with fear to the mother who had already lost two of her boys. "Robert is too young to leave college, he will give more efficient service to his country with a finished education," she pleaded and, with a sigh of relief, she saw that her arguments had won a respite of at least a few more months. Tad, who lived merrily and vitally in the present, could dispel the gloomy thoughts of the past and instill a feeling of youth and hopefulness in the hearts of his parents.

On the first day of January, 1863, Lincoln rewrote the proclamation of emancipation and it was duly signed by him that same afternoon.

The outcry in the North that Mary Lincoln was not in sympathy with her husband in regard to slavery had absolutely no foundation, and when she was accused

of disloyalty to the Union—of corresponding with Secessionists—it hurt her to the quick and she denied herself the privilege of opening any private or personal
letters or packages until they had first been censored.
Mr. Stoddard, in a letter to Dr. Spencer, of Lexington,
Kentucky, calls her "a noble-hearted woman, who was
one of the best friends I ever had. During nearly the
whole of her husband's first term, I was half jocularly
described as her secretary, her constant attendant at all
receptions, public or social, and her advisor in many
affairs. She was a woman much misrepresented and
scandalously abused. For instance, the slanders assail-
ing her patriotism, which was sincere and earnest; ac-
cusations of correspondence with secessionists, etc.
During all that time she would open no letter or parcel
until I had opened and decided whether she should
see it."

Early in April in a raging snowstorm, the President,
Mrs. Lincoln, and Tad visited the Army of the Potomac. Mr. Noah Brooks, who accompanied them, said:
"So thick was the weather and so difficult the naviga-
tion, that we were forced to anchor for the night in a
little cove in the Potomac opposite Indian Head, where
we remained until the following morning. I could not
help thinking that if the Rebels had made a raid on the
Potomac at that time, the capture of the Chief Magis-

trate of the United States would have been a very simple matter. So far as I could see, there were no guards on board the boat and no precautions were taken to guard against surprise."

At General Hooker's headquarters the party was provided with three large hospital tents for their stay of a week, the tents were floored and furnished with camp bedsteads, the fresh crisp air was invigorating, the review of the magnificent army was encouraging, and Tad was having the time of his life. On the outskirts of the cavalry and in charge of a mounted orderly, the spirited Tad rode with his "gray cloak flying in the gusty wind like the plume of Henry of Navarre." The President acknowledged that it was a great relief to get away from Washington and the politicians, but said sadly, "nothing touches the tired spot." A photograph of a Confederate officer came through the lines while Mrs. Lincoln was in camp; it was addressed to General Averill who had been a classmate of the sender and on the back of the photograph was written "A rebellious Rebel." Mrs. Lincoln declared it meant that the rebel officer was in rebellion against the rebel government, but Mr. Lincoln smiled and said, "It means that rebel officer wants everybody to know he is a double-dyed-in-the-wool sort of rebel, a rebel of rebels."

President Lincoln particularly enjoyed the jests of the soldiers. A Confederate soldier jested thus in a Confederate newspaper:

"Our minister nearly got himself into a scrape the other day and whether he is a bit of a wag or a very careless fellow or an 'Abolition traitor' is now the subject of discussion with us. At the meeting on Fast Day he gave out Dr. Watts hymn commencing:

> And are we wretches yet alive
> And do we yet rebel
> 'Tis wondrous, 'tis amazing grace
> That we are out of hell."

The President's family as usual spent the summer months at the Soldiers' Home. There was more fresh air, less formality, and Tad could live on the back of his pony; but no matter how she tried, Mary Lincoln could not ease that "tired spot" in her husband's heart. She saw him with hollows under his eyes and a groping gloomy look out of them which seemed to pierce far into a tragic future. Her own eyes watching him would grow misty with anxiety, seeing which Mr. Lincoln would force a cheering smile and pat the "little woman's" shoulder. They grew closer and more lovingly dependent on each other day by day during these heart-breaking years. While driving out to the Soldiers' Home in July, Mrs. Lincoln was violently thrown from her carriage, and severely injured by her head striking a stone. The President was greatly alarmed and watched over her tenderly and anxiously and overwhelmed the trained nurse with thanks for saving "Mother's" life. He sent this telegram to Robert, a student at Harvard:

"Executive Mansion, Washington
July 3, 1863.

"Robert T. Lincoln
Cambridge, Mass.

Don't be uneasy your mother very slightly hurt by her fall.

A LINCOLN."

In August another shock came to Mary Lincoln. In a skirmish at Baton Rouge, Louisiana, her youngest brother lay silent in his uniform of gray. Surely it couldn't be true! He was so young, only a boy—just about the age of her own son Robert; in his babyhood he had been the darling of her heart, *her* loving, fiery, red-headed brother! In memory she felt his warm, moist little hand clinging affectionately to hers. The romping, merry, warm-hearted little rascal! She could hear his voice with a slight lisp, "See, Sister Mary," as he tried to attract her attention to the merits of his new puppies and, mark of the deepest love and admiration in a small boy's heart, "I am going to let you take your

RODGER NORTH TODD, MARY TODD'S UNCLE, WHO HAD MOVED FROM KENTUCKY TO COLUMBIA, MISSOURI
From an oil portrait painted about 1856

JUDGE DAVID TODD OF COLUMBIA, MISSOURI, MARY TODD'S UNCLE, AT WHOSE HOME SHE HAD A ROMANTIC MEETING WITH ABRAHAM LINCOLN DURING THE WILLIAM HENRY HARRISON CAMPAIGN

The Lincoln Home in Springfield, Illinois

choice of the lot of them, Sister Mary." She read again:

"At the battle of Baton Rouge Lieutenant Alexander H. Todd, aide-de-camp and brother-in-law of General Ben Hardin Helm was killed. He was only twenty-three years of age, full of promise, of handsome appearance and winning manners, and idolized by his mother and sisters."

Mary Lincoln fell on her knees and wept, "Oh, little Aleck, why had you too to die!" She must still her sobs, her tears must be shed bravely, in secret, there must be no suspicion that she grieved for a dead Confederate soldier—for her husband's sake, as well as for her own, she must not risk the title of traitor—she must control her paroxysm of grief and assume a smile. Her husband would know and understand. No gossiping tongue would tell an unsympathetic world of her sorrow for her dead Confederate brothers. This shock more than her fall retarded Mary Lincoln's recovery. Mr. Lincoln replied to a telegram which came from one of Mary Lincoln's girlhood friends and a near relative of her stepmother:

"Washington, D. C.
August 21, 1863.

"Mrs. Margaret Preston
Lexington, Kentucky.

Your dispatch to Mrs. L. received yesterday. She is not well. Owing to her early and strong friendship for you I would gladly oblige you, but I cannot absolutely do it. If General Bogle and Hon. James Guthrie one or both in their discretion see fit to give you the passes, this is my authority to them for doing so.

A. LINCOLN."

Mrs. Lincoln and Tad went to New York. Mrs. Lincoln had recovered her health so slowly and looked so pallid that in September, before her return to Washington, her husband became very anxious.

"War Department Washington
September 21, 1863.

"Mrs. A. Lincoln
Fifth Avenue Hotel,
New York.

The air is so clear and cold and apparently healthy that I would be glad for you to come. Nothing very particular but I would be glad to see you and Tad.

A. LINCOLN."

"New York
September 21, 1863.

"Edward McManus
Executive Mansion.

Go to Col. McCullum and ask him to send the green car on to Philadelphia for me and make arrangements for a

special car from New York to Philadelphia. Send me a
reply immediately.

Mrs. Lincoln."

"Executive Mansion, Washington
September 22, 1863.

"Mrs. A. Lincoln
Fifth Avenue Hotel,
New York.

   Did you receive my dispatch of yesterday? Mrs. Cuth-
bert did not correctly understand me I directed her to tell
you to use your own pleasure whether to stay or come; and
I did not say it is sickly and that you should on no account
come. So far as I see or know, it was never healthier and
I really wish to see you. Answer this on receipt.

A. Lincoln."

"New York
September 22, 1863.

"A. Lincoln:
   Your telegram received. Did you not receive my reply?
I have telegraphed Col. McCullum to have the car ready
at the earliest possible moment. Have a very bad cold
and am anxious to return home as you may suppose. Taddie
is well.

Mrs. Lincoln."

   But before the car was ready, she received distressing
news in another telegram:

"War Department, Washington
September 24, 1863.

"Mrs. A. Lincoln
Fifth Avenue Hotel,
New York.

We now have a tolerable accurate summing up of the late battle between Rosecrans and Bragg. The result is that we are worsted if at all only in the fact that we after the main fighting was over, yielded the ground, thus leaving considerable of our artillery and wounded to fall into the enemy's hands for which we got nothing in turn. We lost in general officers one killed and three or four wounded— all brigadiers; whilst according to rebel accounts which we have, they lost six killed and eight wounded. Of the killed one Major General and five brigadiers including your brother-in-law Helm, and of the wounded three Major Generals and five brigadiers. This list may be reduced in number by correction of confusion in names. At 11:40 a.m. yesterday General Rosecrans telegraphs from Chattanooga 'We hold this point, and I cannot be dislodged except by very superior numbers and a great battle.' A dispatch leaving there after night yesterday says 'No fight to-day.'
A. LINCOLN."

"I never saw Mr. Lincoln more moved," said Senator David Davis, "than when he heard of the death of his young brother-in-law Ben Hardin Helm, only thirty-two years old, at Chickamauga. I called to see him about four o'clock on the 22nd of September; I found

him in the greatest grief. 'Davis,' said he, 'I feel as
David of old did when he was told of the death of
Absalom.' I saw how grief stricken he was so I closed
the door and left him alone." (From the Washington
Post.)

Mary Lincoln did rejoice at the Union victories, but,
oh, what a price to pay! Not even the poor consolation
of open sorrow for her dear dead! She must hide from
prying, suspicious, and unsympathetic eyes every evidence of grief at the blotting out of a Conferedate soldier no matter how near and dear to her, or be branded
as a traitor to her country and hang as a millstone
around the neck of her adored husband. Grieving in-
consolably over the death of her little son, she shed
many a secret and bitter tear for her fine young
brothers.

The Northerners had no sympathy for a Southern-
born woman whose brothers were in the rebel army.
They watched her suspiciously for a sign of disloyalty.
She knew that a single tear shed for a dead enemy
would bring torrents of scorn and bitter abuse on both
her husband and herself.

On the other hand, the Southerners shouted that she
was hard-hearted, callous, indifferent to the sufferings
of her own people; so flinty-hearted that she showed no
emotion, not even a trace of feeling at the loss of her

brothers and friends. Sneered at, hated, buffeted by both sides, could any position be more brimful of anguish? Sometimes, feeling that she had not a friend left on earth, Mary gallantly held her proud head high, and erect, poised, and dignified, she hid her private griefs and entertained at the White House only when it seemed obligatory.

"It was a remarkable fact," says Frank Carpenter, "that she was less hospitable than any previous mistress of the White House. No one could ascertain the reason why." To anyone knowing these facts and having an understanding heart, the reason is plain to see.

CHAPTER X

"SEND HER TO ME"

ALTHOUGH three weeks had passed since the fierce battle of Chickamauga on September 20, 1863, Governor Helm, of Kentucky, had only just received the news of the death of General Ben Hardin Helm, his son and Mrs. Todd's son-in-law. The governor wrote the following letter to Mrs. Robert S. Todd, of Lexington:

"Elizabethtown Ky
October 11, 1863.

"Dear Madam:

It is due to you that I announce the death of my son. He fell in the battle south of Chattanooga I have unquestionable information. He was buried at Atlanta. It is probable Emilie was there. Could you through friends or by your own relationship secure for Emilie a passport home. If she could be allowed to come to Nashville I would go after her, if a pass would be allowed me. I am totally at a loss to know how to begin. Could you or one of your daughters write to Mrs. Lincoln and through her secure a pass?

In deep sorrow
I am respectfully,
JOHN L. HELM."

219

Mrs. Helm, who had been summoned from Selma, Alabama, to Atlanta, Georgia, by General Braxton Bragg, C. S. A., arrived there only in time for the last sad rites over her soldier husband. General Bragg promised to appeal to General U. S. Grant for a passport for Mrs. Helm to return to Kentucky, for she was longing for her native State and for the comforting arms of her mother. After a week in Atlanta some Kentucky friends who were living at that time in Madison, Georgia, urged Mrs. Helm to come to them until the arrival of the hoped-for pass which, although she did not know it at that time, General Grant had already refused to give her. In the meantime Mrs. Todd had secured passes from President Lincoln permitting her to go South and bring her daughter home.

The pass reads:

"To Whom It May Concern:

"It is my wish that Mrs. Emilie T. Helm (Widow of the late B. H. Helm, who fell in the Confederate service) now returning to Kentucky, may have protection of person and property except as to slaves of which I say nothing.

A. LINCOLN."

When Mrs. Helm reached Fortress Monroe she was told that she could not proceed to Kentucky without taking the oath of allegiance to the United States. Distressed, heart-broken as she was and fearing that she might be sent back South, alone and almost penniless, she firmly refused to take the oath. It was treason to her dead husband, to her beloved Southland. The Federal officers argued with her kindly, but in vain. They could not disobey this order even for the sister-in-law of the President. One of them, at last, at his wit's end, said, "We will have to telegraph the President your decision." After a few hours of anxious and trembling suspense, Mrs. Helm saw the officer re-appear smiling and waving a telegram in his hand. She took it and read:

"Send her to me.

A. LINCOLN."

Greatly relieved, Mrs. Helm proceeded to Washington. Mrs. Lincoln's young sister Emilie was a pathetic little figure in her trailing black crêpe. It made Mary Lincoln's heart ache and her eyes fill with tears to think of the sorrow that in three years could change the rosy, laughing Emilie into this sad-faced girl with pallid cheeks, tragic eyes, and tight unsmiling lips. Quoting from Mrs. Helm's diary:

"Mr. Lincoln and my sister met me with the warmest affection, we were all too grief-stricken at first for speech. I have lost my husband, they have lost their fine little son Willie and Mary and I have lost three brothers in the Confederate service. We could only embrace each other in silence and tears. Sister and I dined intimately, alone. Our tears gathered silently and fell unheeded as with choking voices we tried to talk of immaterial things. We talked of old friends in Springfield and in Kentucky. Allusion to the present is like tearing open a fresh and bleeding wound and the pain is too great for self-control. And the future, alas, the future seems empty, of everything but despair. So to gain anything like calmness we approach any subject timidly and wonder if anything we are about to say can give the other pain. After dinner sister had the East room and the Green and Blue rooms lighted up for me to see. The Red room is the usual drawing room and contains the portrait of Washington which Dolly Madison cut out of the frame to save from the British. Dolly Madison's first husband was a Todd.

"The room I occupied had been fitted up for the visit of the Prince of Wales. The purple hangings seem gloomy and funereal though brightened with yellow cords.

"General Sickles called. He has lost one leg and goes on crutches. He seems on very intimate terms here.

"It is quite cold although only November and a fire is cheerful and comfortable.

"There is an expedition to the Russian fleet and all the members of Congress have gone to it.

"Sister is doing everything to distract my mind and her own from our terrible grief, but at times it overwhelms us; we can't get away from it, try as we will to be cheerful and accept fate. Sister has always a cheerful word and a smile for Mr. Lincoln, who seems thin and care-worn and seeing her sorrowful would add to his care.

"Driving out in the state carriage to-day, we came suddenly on a street car from which some little boys were jumping. Our driver was unable to stop his horses in time, and the carriage ran over a little boy, breaking his leg. Sister Mary, distressed and excited, jumped out of the carriage, crying, 'Oh, the poor baby! Who is he, where does he live? I will take him to his mother.' She started to lift him up in her arms, but a doctor who happened to be in the crowd which had quickly collected, said, 'No, Mrs. Lincoln, you had better let me handle him. I will take him home.' So we followed to the child's home, Mary to tell the mother how distressed she is over the unavoidable accident and to beg to be allowed to do everything possible for the little fellow. She at once sent fruit and flowers and has promised the little boy to bring him some toys to-morrow. Mary mothers all children.

"We called again to-day on the little invalid with toys, fruit and a box of candy. He is a brave little fellow, his eyes glisten when he sees us coming and he forgets he has a broken leg in his pleasure over his toys.

"Sister and I cannot open our hearts to each other as freely as we would like. This frightful war comes between us like a barrier of granite closing our lips but not our hearts, for though our tongues are tied, we weep over our dead together and express through our clasped hands the sympathy we feel for each other in our mutual grief.

"Sister Mary and I avoid any reference to the war or to any of my experiences in the South for fear of hurting each other. Her fine tact and delicacy fill me with admiration. She can so quickly turn a dangerous subject into other channels.

"We were talking of mother to-day and Sister sent her many messages of love and sympathy: 'My heart bleeds for her, Emilie,' said she, 'a wound in a mother's heart can never heal. I pray God you will never have that sorrow to bear.' Sister Mary's heart is particularly sore over the death of Alec. He was so young, so loving, so impetuous, our dear, red-headed, baby brother!

"Sister Mary's tenderness for me is very touching. She and Brother Lincoln pet me as if I were a child, and, without words, try to comfort me.

"Sister Mary was sitting in a drooping despondent attitude as I came across the room to kiss her good morning; the newspaper she had been reading dropped to the floor as she held her arms out to me and said, 'Kiss me, Emilie, and tell me that you love me! I seem to be the scape-goat for both North and South!' Then suddenly as if she had thrown off a dark cloak and stood revealed in a gay costume, she held her head up and smiled. I was marveling at the transformation but instantly understood the cause as Brother Lincoln's voice came to us, 'I hope you two are planning some mischief.' Mischief!—I am sure he saw Mary's despondency and heard what she said to me and that his cheerfulness was forced, for later in the day he said: 'Little Sister, I hope you can come up and spend the summer with us at the Soldiers' Home, you and Mary love each other—it is good for her to have you with her—I feel worried about Mary, her nerves have gone to pieces; she cannot hide from me that the strain she has been under has been too much for her mental as well as her physical health. What do you think?' he asked me anxiously. I answered him as I knew he wished me to do, candidly. 'She seems very nervous and excitable and once or twice when I have come into the room suddenly the frightened look in her eyes has appalled me. She seems to fear that other sorrows may be added to those we already have to bear. I believe if anything should happen to you or Robert or Tad it would kill her.' Brother Lincoln said, as he shook his head sorrowfully: 'Stay with her as long as you can.'

"Later in the day Sister Mary asked me, 'Emilie, what do you think of Mr. Lincoln, do you think he is well?' I really think he looks very ill, but I only answered, 'He seems thinner than I ever saw him.' 'Oh, Emilie, will we ever awake from this hideous nightmare?' she exclaimed. I did not answer, for it does not seem possible we ever can.

"After I had said good night and had gone to my room last night there was a gentle knock at the door, and Sister Mary's voice, 'Emilie, may I come in?' She was smiling though her eyes were full of tears. 'I want to tell you, Emilie, that one may not be wholly without comfort when our loved ones leave us. When my noble little Willie was first taken from me, I felt that I had fallen into a deep pit of gloom and despair without a ray of light anywhere. If I had not felt the spur of necessity urging me to cheer Mr. Lincoln, whose grief was as great as my own, I could never have smiled again, and if Willie did not come to comfort me I would still be drowned in tears, and while I long inexpressibly to touch him, to hold him in my arms, and still grieve that he has no future in this world that I might watch with a proud mother's heart—he lives, Emilie!' she said with a thrill in her voice I can never forget. 'He comes to me every night, and stands at the foot of my bed with the same sweet, adorable smile he has always had; he does not always come alone; little Eddie is sometimes with him and twice he has come with our brother Alec, he tells me he loves his Uncle Alec and is with him most of the time. You cannot dream of the comfort this gives me. When I thought of my little son in immensity, alone, without his mother to direct him, no one to hold his little hand in loving guidance, it nearly broke my heart.' Sister Mary's eyes were wide and shining and I had a feeling of awe as if I were in the presence of the supernatural.

"It *is* unnatural and abnormal, it frightens me. It does not seem like Sister Mary to be so nervous and wrought up. She is on a terrible strain and her smiles seem forced. She is frightened about Robert going into the Army. She said to-day to Brother Lincoln (I was reading in another part of the room but could not help hearing the conversation): 'Of course, Mr. Lincoln, I know that Robert's plea to go into the Army is manly and noble and I want him to go, but oh! I am so frightened he may never come back to us!"

"Mr. Lincoln said sadly, 'Many a poor mother, Mary, has had to make this sacrifice and has given up every son she had—and lost them all.' 'Don't I know that only too well?' cried Mary; 'before this war is ended I may be like that poor mother, like my poor mother in Kentucky, with not a prop left in her old age.' I heard no more, for feeling the conversation was not meant for me to hear I left the room.

"Cousin John Stuart (Hon. John T. Stuart, of Springfield, Illinois) is here. In his manner of greeting me he could not have been more deferential and courtly if he had been bending over the royal hand of Queen Victoria. In his avoidance of any reference to my bereavement he shows his gentle kindness. I have always loved and admired him—more than ever now since the episode of last night when I was conscious his gentle sympathetic eyes were urging me to be patient.

"Seeing some cards being handed to Sister Mary and hearing the callers were to be received in the room where we were sitting, I excused myself and slipped out. In a few minutes Sister Mary sent for me to come and see some friend who wished especially to see me that he might inquire about some mutual friend in the South. I went most reluctantly. It is painful to see friends and I do not feel like meeting strangers. I cannot bear their inquiring look at my deep crêpe. It was General Sickles again, calling with Senator Harris. General Sickles said, 'I told Senator Harris that

BEN HARDIN HELM
Cadet at West Point, graduate of class of 1851. Married
Emilie Todd

MARY TODD'S SISTER ELODIE, WHO MARRIED COLONEL N. H. R. DAWSON OF
SELMA, ALABAMA

you were at the White House, just from the South and
could probably give him some news of his old friend
General John C. Breckinridge.' I told Senator Harris
that as I had not seen General Breckinridge for some
time I could give him no news of the general's health.
He then asked me several pointed questions about the
South and as politely as I could I gave him non-com-
mittal answers. Senator Harris said to me in a voice
of triumph, 'Well, we have whipped the rebels at Chattanooga and I hear, madam, that the scoundrels ran
like scared rabbits.' 'It was the example, Senator
Harris, that you set them at Bull Run and Manassas,'
I answered with a choking throat. I was very nervous
and I could see that Sister Mary was annoyed. She
tactfully tried to change the subject, whereupon Senator Harris turned to her abruptly and with an unsmiling face asked sternly: 'Why isn't Robert in the Army?
He is old enough and strong enough to serve his country. He should have gone to the front some time ago.'

"Sister Mary's face turned white as death and I saw
that she was making a desperate effort at self-control.
She bit her lip, but answered quietly, 'Robert is making
his preparations now to enter the Army, Senator Harris; he is not a shirker as you seem to imply for he
has been anxious to go for a long time. If fault there
be, it is mine, I have insisted that he should stay in

college a little longer as I think an educated man can serve his country with more intelligent purpose than an ignoramus.' General Harris rose and said harshly and pointedly to Sister, 'I have only one son and he is fighting for his country.' Turning to me and making a low bow, 'And, Madam, if I had twenty sons they should all be fighting the rebels.' 'And if I had twenty sons, General Harris,' I replied, 'they should all be opposing yours.' I forgot where I was, I forgot that I was a guest of the President and Mrs. Lincoln at the White House. I was cold and trembling. I stumbled out of the room somehow, for I was blinded by tears and my heart was beating to suffocation. Before I reached the privacy of my room where unobserved I could give way to my grief, Sister Mary overtook me and put her arms around me. I felt somehow comforted to weep on her shoulder—her own tears were falling but she said no word of the occurrence and I understood that she was powerless to protect a guest in the White House from cruel rudeness.

"Cousin John Stuart told me that after I left the room and General Sickles and Senator Harris, on their way out, had reached the portico of the White House, that General Sickles had painfully stumped up the stairs again and declared he must see the President, who had not been feeling well and was in his own room lying down. When the President came in General Sickles solemnly related the conversation between General Harris and myself, the President's eyes twinkled and he looked at Cousin John and chuckled, 'The child has a tongue like the rest of the Todds.'

"This seemed to anger General Sickles and he said in a loud, dictatorial voice, slapping the table with his hand, 'You should not have that rebel in your house.'

Mr. Lincoln instantly drew himself up and said in a quiet, dignified voice, 'Excuse me, General Sickles, my wife and I are in the habit of choosing our own guests. We do not need from our friends either advice or assistance in the matter. Besides,' he added, 'the little "rebel" came because I ordered her to come, it was not of her own volition.'

"This is the only time a word of the war has been spoken—in my presence or to me—since I have been in the White House; it is most considerate. Although Brother Lincoln and Sister Mary have urged me to stay longer, I feel that my being here is more or less an embarrassment to all of us and I am longing for Kentucky and Mother. They have both (Mary and Mr. Lincoln) invited me to make them a long visit next summer at the Soldiers' Home. It is kind of them—but it will not be possible.

"I had my little daughter with me. Tad, who was

five or six years older, was playing host and entertaining her with photographs, both seated on the rug before the fire. He showed her a photograph of himself with great pride and then picking up one of his father, said, 'This is the President.' My little daughter looked at it, shook her head and said very emphatically, 'No, that is not the President, Mr. Davis is President.' Tad, to make his statement more emphatic, shouted, 'Hurrah for Abe Lincoln.' My little daughter defiantly replied, 'Hurrah for Jeff Davis.' Mr. Lincoln listened with an amused smile to the heated argument and when finally appealed to by Tad, he said, 'Well, Tad, you know who is your President, and I am your little cousin's Uncle Lincoln.' So, taking one on each knee, he pacified the tense and glaring little belligerents.

"I was at the White House nearly a week. As Mr. Lincoln handed me the safeguard, the paper protecting me from molestation except as to slaves, he looked at me earnestly and said gravely, 'Little Sister, I never knew you to do a mean thing in your life. I know you will not embarrass me in any way on your return to Kentucky.' Nothing was said to me then or afterwards about taking the oath of allegiance. Brother Lincoln knew, that, while under the circumstances this for me would be impossible, he could trust my honor to do nothing to make him regret his loving kindness and consideration for me. They were, both Sister Mary and Mr. Lincoln, careful not to allude to politics or to the South, or in any way to hurt me or make it difficult for me.

"Mr. Lincoln in the intimate talks we had was very much affected over the misfortunes of our family; and of my husband he said, 'You know, Little Sister, I tried to have Ben come with me. I hope you do not feel any bitterness or that I am in any way to blame for all this sorrow.' I answered it was 'the fortune of war' and that while my husband loved him and had been deeply grateful to him for his generous offer to make him an officer in the Federal Army, he had to follow his conscience and that for weal or woe he felt he must side with his own people. Mr. Lincoln put his arms around me and we both wept."

CHAPTER XI

"New York
December 4, 1863.

"Abraham Lincoln
President United States.

Reached here last evening. Very tired and severe headache. Hope to hear you are doing well. Expect a telegraph to-day.

Mrs. Lincoln."

"Executive Mansion, Washington
December 5, 1863.

"Mrs. A. Lincoln
Metropolitan Hotel,
New York.

All doing well.

A. Lincoln."

"New York,
December 6, 1863.

"A. Lincoln

Do let me know immediately how Taddie and yourself
are. I will be home by Tuesday without fail; sooner if
needed.

Mrs. Lincoln."

Not receiving a prompt reply although a telegram

had been sent "All doing well," Mrs. Lincoln anxiously sent another telegram the same day.

> "New York
> December 6, 1863.

"Edward McManus
Executive Mansion

Let me know immediately exactly how Mr. Lincoln and Taddie are.

> MRS. LINCOLN
> Metropolitan Hotel."

> "Executive Mansion, Washington
> December 7, 1863.

"Mrs. A. Lincoln
Metropolitan Hotel,
New York.

All doing well Tad confidently expects you to-night when will you come?

> A. LINCOLN."

> "New York
> December 7, 1863.

"A. Lincoln

Will leave here positively at 8 a. m. Tuesday morning. Have carriage waiting at depot in Washington at 6 p. m. Did Tad receive his book. Please answer.

> MRS. LINCOLN."

"Executive Mansion, Washington
December 7, 1863.

"Mrs. A. Lincoln
Metropolitan Hotel,
New York.

Tad has received his book. The carriage shall be ready at 6 p. m. tomorrow.

A. LINCOLN."

In the early months of 1864, while some politicians were in favor of a more radical man, there grew a popular demand for the renomination of President Lincoln, which by the time of the convention was so universal as to overwhelm all opposition. The prospect of the preservation of the Union brought to Lincoln's heart the hope that kindness in reconstruction would weld the two sections together again in brotherly love. This hope may have reconciled him to continuing the great burden of his high office, of which he had said: "If to be the head of Hell is as hard as what I have to undergo here I could find it in my heart to pity Satan himself."

The souls of President and Mrs. Lincoln at the pinnacle of their ambition were filled with weariness. Mr. Carpenter, the artist, seeing the tired droop of the President, suggested that he was working too hard, and Lincoln replied, "I can't work less—but it is not that—work never troubled me. Things look bad and I can't avoid anxiety. Personally I care nothing about a reëlection; but if our divisions defeat us I fear for the country." When Carpenter suggested that right must eventually triumph, that he had never despaired of the result, Mr. Lincoln said sadly, "Neither have I, but I may never live to see it. I feel a presentiment that I shall not outlast the Rebellion. When it is over, my work will be done."

Mary Lincoln saw with deep solicitude his dear face grow pinched and more and more furrowed with sharply cut lines of care, and the deep-set gray eyes sink to hollows of sadness. Responsibility, care, anxiety, the disasters of the army, the injustice and dis-affection of the friends he had trusted, were wearing away his nerves of steel. His giant frame was almost emaciated, and he seemed to stoop with weariness; the ready, spontaneous laugh of earlier days was seldom heard and his infrequent smiles did not seem to come from his heart. He said one day, "I feel as though I shall never be glad any more." His wife made any excuse to draw him away from his labors—she needed a drive, wouldn't he go with her?—or a plea which never failed, wouldn't he accompany her to some hospital to cheer the sick soldiers? Mrs. Lincoln was so constant in her visits to the hospitals, so gentle in her efforts to minister to and cheer the sick soldiers, that she was derisively styled by the Southern papers "The Yankee nurse." Secretary Seward, Senator Sumner, and other friends aided her in her efforts to divert the President's mind from the pressure of his arduous duties, and he often rode or walked with them but returned to the White House to the same old routine of business—answering telegrams, making momentous decisions.

Although General Grant had relieved the President of much of his anxious responsibility in the conduct of the war, and there was every reason to think the struggle would soon be over, there loomed the difficult problem of reconstruction. His political anxieties, too, were greater than they had been since the beginning of the war.

No matter what misfortune overtook them, Mary and her husband were sure of their love and loyalty for each other which had never flagged since Mr. Lincoln had placed on Mary's finger the ring which bore on its inner circle, "Love is eternal." They made pathetic efforts to cheer each other, and Tad must have no share in war-time gloom.

"New York City
April 28, 1864.

"Hon. A. Lincoln
President United States.

We reached here in safety. Hope you are well. Please send me by mail to-day a check for $50 directed to me, care Mr. Warren Leland, Metropolitan Hotel, Tad says are the goats well.

MRS. LINCOLN."

"Executive Mansion, Washington
April 28, 1864.

"Mrs. A. Lincoln
Metropolitan Hotel,
New York.

The draft will go to you. Tell Tad the goats and father are very well—especially the goats.

A. LINCOLN."

When away from each other the telegrams went over the wires sometimes twice a day.

The Union Convention met in June, and President Lincoln received the news of his renomination without elation. To the delegation which came to congratulate him, he said, "I do not allow myself to suppose that either the convention or the League have concluded to decide that I am either the greatest or the best man in America, but rather they have concluded it is not best to swap horses while crossing the river * * *."

"Executive Mansion, Washington
June 24, 1864.

"Mrs. A. Lincoln
Boston, Mass.

All well and very warm.   Tad and I have been to General
Grant's Army.   Returned yesterday safe and sound.

A. LINCOLN."

"War Department, Washington
August 31, 1864.

"Mrs. A. Lincoln
Manchester, Vermont.

All reasonably well.   Bob is not here yet.   How is dear
Tad?

A. LINCOLN."

In July and August Washington was passing
through its deepest days of gloom. No joyful tiding
from General Grant cheered the hearts of the Unionists who had so lately shouted that victory was close
at hand, and politics were in a very chaotic state.   The
President wrote the following memorandum dated August 23, 1864.   "This morning as for some days past
it seems exceedingly probable that this administration
will not be reëlected.   Then it will be my duty to so
coöperate with the President elect as to save the Union
between the election and the inauguration * * *."

Mrs. Lincoln was not well and Washington was un-
bearably warm.

"War Department, Washington
September 8, 1864.

"Mrs. A. Lincoln
Manchester, Vermont.

All well including Tad's pony and the goats. Mrs.
Colonel Demmick died night before last. Bob left Sunday
afternoon said he did not know whether he should see you.

A. LINCOLN."

Both Mr. and Mrs. Lincoln were fatalists. In the
case of threats of his assassination, the President was
passive, accepting, but never taking of his own accord,
measures to prevent what he considered might be a
preordained destiny. Mary would fight fate to the
last gasp; though nervous and frightened, she would
be happier to die fighting. That she felt the menace
of death hanging over the President's head and had a
constant fear of attack, the following will show.

Mrs. Mary B. Clay, a daughter of Cassius M. Clay,
minister to the court of Russia, relates in the Lexington, Kentucky, *Herald* an incident which happened in
the winter of 1865:

"Our Uncle Brutus J. Clay invited my sister and
myself to visit him in Washington, he being Congressman at that time. Mrs. Ninian Edwards (born Elizabeth Todd) and Mrs. Lincoln (born Mary Todd)
were intimate childhood friends of my mother, Mary

Jane Warfield Clay, Elizabeth Todd being one of her bridesmaids, so that when we arrived in Washington we sent our cards to Mrs. Lincoln who soon sent her carriage for us to come to see her. The Lady of the White House at that time made no calls upon anyone, but took her friends driving, invited them to see her or to go with her to the theater, concerts, etc. Mrs. Lincoln invited us to go with her to Ford's Theatre one night, sending the carriage to take us to the White House thence to the theater. President and Mrs. Lincoln, my sister and myself occupied one carriage. Mr. Nicolay and John Hay went in another with a guard of eight men, I believe on horseback, which had been voted by Congress to escort and guard Mr. Lincoln.

"As we drove along, the carriage being swung very low, an iron hoop was caught under it and pierced through the seat, coming through between Mr. and Mrs. Lincoln who occupied the back seat. Mrs. Lincoln was very much alarmed and feared an attack was being made. The hoop was removed and we proceeded on our way. I said to Mr. Lincoln, 'What do you think of this guard as a protection?' 'Not much,' he said, 'for I believe when my time comes there is nothing that can prevent my going, but the people will have it.' When we stopped at the theater the pavement about the door was packed with people. The

guard made a way for us into the theater and I thought
as we passed that an assassin might easily kill the President in that crowd and escape detection.

"In the theater President and Mrs. Lincoln, Miss
Sallie Clay and I, Mr. Nicolay and Mr. Hay, occupied
the same box which the year after saw Mr. Lincoln
slain by Booth.   I do not recall the play, but Wilkes
Booth played the part of villain.   The box was right
on the stage, with a railing around it.   Mr. Lincoln sat
next to the rail, I next to Mrs. Lincoln, Miss Sallie
Clay and the other gentlemen farther around.   Twice
Booth in uttering disagreeable threats in the play came
very near and put his finger close to Mr. Lincoln's
face; when he came a third time I was impressed by
it, and said, 'Mr. Lincoln, he looks as if he meant that
for you.'   'Well,' he said, 'he does look pretty sharp
at me, doesn't he?'   At the same theater, the next April,
Wilkes Booth shot our dear President.   Mr. Lincoln
looked to me the personification of honesty, and when
animated was much better looking than his pictures
represent him.

"Mrs. Lincoln was a very proud woman, and the
wives of the senators and committees who visited Mrs.
Lincoln on her arrival to induct her into the formali-
ties of the White House made a mistake in the woman
they were to meet in Mr. Lincoln's wife.   All her life

accustomed to the best society, she resented that any one should suppose that she would not know how to conduct herself as the wife of the President; she resented their mistaken kindness, made enemies of them, and never recovered their friendship.

"Mrs. Senator Zack Chandler, who was one of these mistaken ones, told me the trouble was, they took for granted that Lincoln had married a woman in what they supposed would be his position in life, and without waiting to see and know Mrs. Lincoln and then give her advice if she needed it, they made that fatal step—a most unfortunate one; and it was I think, the origin of the unpopularity of Mrs. Lincoln."

March 4, 1865, the day of Lincoln's second inauguration, was a somber, cloudy, drizzly day as gloomy as the day of his second election in November. In spite of the mud under foot, ladies in fine apparel were to be seen in large numbers in the crowds which thronged the streets leading to the Capitol.

Poor Andrew Johnson, Vice President elect, with a red face, arm in arm with Hannibal Hamlin, was noticeably tipsy and during his long and incoherent harangue President Lincoln sat patiently listening. Mary Lincoln, who had been escorted to the inaugural ceremonies by Senator Harlan, sat in the diplomatic gallery. She shared all the sensations which affected the audience of that embarrassing occasion; like Staunton, she was petrified—then blushed with shame for him as did Senator Henry Wilson; Senator Sumner's face wore a sarcastic smile, and Judge Nelson of the Supreme Bench was plainly horrified.

This painful scene finally over, the procession formed for the inauguration platform. President Lincoln, tall and gaunt, his rugged features earnest and sad, rose to deliver his inaugural address. Mary Lincoln's heart thrilled with pride. She exultantly acquiesced in the closing words—so touching and memorable:

"With malice towards none, with charity for all, with firmness in the right as God gives us to see the right, let us strive to finish the work we are in, to bind up the nation's wounds, to care for him who shall have borne the battle and for his widow, and his orphans—to do all which may achieve and cherish a just and lasting peace among ourselves and with all nations."

When Mary returned to the White House after the inauguration ceremonies were over, she was calmer and less expectant of the lurking death she feared might be lying in wait for her husband, than she had been since the morning they left Springfield. In the retrospect, how peaceful and happy was that modest

home on the corner of Eighth and Jackson Streets—
that small white house with its green shutters! Did she
wish she had never left it? She, as well as her husband, had a "tired spot" that could not be rested, but
now they were buoyed up by the hope that in another
four years they with their two sons could settle down
to a quiet, carefree, domestic life. Of course, Mr. Lincoln was proud, and so was Mary, that the people had
selected him again as their Chief Magistrate.

With a smiling face hiding her private griefs from
the public and assuming a cheerfulness she could not
feel, to comfort her husband, Mary Lincoln planned
with him what to do with life when they left Washington. Travel first; in seeing foreign countries they
could forget for a time their sorrows and the terrible
excitement of the war; then a quiet, peaceful home in
Springfield where they could end their days among
loving friends.

The President, urged by his wife and friends, decided to take a much-needed holiday, the first he had
taken since he entered the White House in 1861. He
went to City Point to the headquarters of General
Grant, accompanied by a party of friends among whom
were Senator James Harlan and his wife and their
young daughter Mary (who a few years later became

the wife of Robert Todd Lincoln), Senator Sumner, the Marquis de Chambrun, and a number of others, and before going notified Robert, who had graduated from Harvard and was a volunteer officer on General Grant's staff.

> "War Department, Washington
> March 21, 1865.

"Capt. Robert T. Lincoln
City Point, Va.

We now think of starting to you about 1 p. m. Thursday. Don't make public.

> A. LINCOLN."

This was the last visit that the President, Mrs. Lincoln, and Tad paid to the Army of the Potomac. A week later the President telegraphed the Secretary of War: "I begin to feel that I ought to be at home." And Mr. Stanton replied, "I hope you will stay to see it out for a few days at least." They were still in Virginia on the first day of April.

> "City Point, Virginia
> April 1, 1865, 1 p. m.

"Hon. Edwin M. Stanton
Secretary of War.

Mrs. Lincoln has started home, and I will thank you to see that our coachman is at the Arsenal Wharf at 8 o'clock to-morrow morning, there to wait until she arrives.

> A. LINCOLN."

"War Department, Washington
April 2, 1865, 11 a. m.

"The President
City Point.

Mrs. Lincoln arrived safely this morning. General Augurs headquarters were burned up last night. Whether the fire was caused by negligence or design is unknown. I congratulate you and General Grant upon the prospect of great success. Every one is eager for news.

EDWIN M. STANTON, Secretary of War."

"City Point, Va.
April 2, 1865, 8:30 a. m.

"Mrs. A. Lincoln
Executive Mansion.

Last night General Grant telegraphed that General Sheridan with his cavalry and the Fifth Corps had captured three brigades of infantry, a train of wagons and several batteries, prisoners amounting to several thousand. This morning General Grant having ordered an attack along the whole line telegraphs as follows . . . Robert yesterday wrote a little cheerful note to Captain Penrose which is all he has heard of him since you left.

A. LINCOLN."

Mrs. Lincoln left Tad with his father, and the President took the excited little fellow with him to Petersburg and Richmond.

"City Point, Va.
April 2, 1865.

"Mrs. Lincoln.

At 4:30 p. m. to-day General Grant telegraphs me that he has Petersburg completely enveloped from river below to river above and has captured since he started last Wednesday about 12,000 prisoners and 50 guns. He suggests that I shall go out and see him in the morning, which I think I will do. Tad and I are both well, and will be glad to see you and your party here at the time you name.

A. LINCOLN."

Mrs. Lincoln, while she was at City Point, was driving one day in April with her husband along the banks of the James River. They came to a country graveyard; the trees surrounding it were just waking from their winter nap and were clothing themselves in tender green. Within the enclosure, the shrubs planted by loving hands were bursting into masses of pink and white blossoms as if to say exultantly, There is no death! this is only a quiet place to rest and sleep!—and the James River seemed to be murmuring a soothing lullaby. Mr. Lincoln ordered the carriage to stop, he and his wife walked through the quiet, peaceful spot, and Mr. Lincoln seemed impressed with its restfulness. "Mary," he said, "you are younger than I. You will survive me. When I am gone, lay my remains in some quiet place like this."

The latter part of March, 1865, Mrs. Ben Hardin Helm and her friend Mrs. Pratt obtained passes to go to Richmond to see about some bales of cotton in which they had invested and which they feared might be lost.

On Mrs. Helm's arrival at Richmond General Singleton, a peace commissioner, advised her to return immediately on the next flag of truce boat as the fall of Richmond was imminent.

General Ord assigned Captain Robert Lincoln to escort two ladies (he did not say who they were) from Fortress Monroe as far as the flag of truce boat could proceed, which was near Petersburg. As a dapper young captain came on board, Mrs. Helm heard an astonished exclamation, "Well, if it isn't my Aunt Emilie!" Simultaneously she exclaimed, "Robert! Oh, how glad I am to see you!" Mrs. Helm was worried at the account Robert gave her of her sister's health. "I think mother has never quite recovered from the effects of her fall," he told his aunt. "It is really astonishing what a brave front she manages to keep when we know she is suffering—most women would be in bed groaning, but not mother! She just straightens herself up a little more and says, 'It is better to laugh than be sighing.' Tad would go all to pieces if she reversed the words of that opera, and so would my father."

"3014 N Street
Washington, D. C.
April 14, 1924.

My dear Aunt Emilie:

Your letter brings to my memory very vividly my putting
you on a pass going south just before the great surrender at
Appomattox. I cannot help thinking of it all now, for I
myself arrived at the White House only a few days later,
and on the day of my arrival my father met his death, so it
seems to me to be a time of very sad memories.

Most affectionately,

ROBERT T. LINCOLN."

In a letter from Robert Todd Lincoln to his aunt
(Mrs. Ben Hardin Helm) he tells of a curious freak
of fate in the lives of the Lincoln family:

"In 1863 or 1864 I started from New York to Washington taking at Jersey City a midnight train. Standing in the station having a sleeping car, the stone
platform was level with the car platform on which
stood a conductor selling berth tickets to a line of passengers who stood leaning against the side of the car.
The line made quite a little crowd of which I was one.
Suddenly the train began to move and by the motion
and the crowding of my neighbors I was screwed off
my feet, which dropped into the slot between the car
and the platform—not very far but the situation was

very dangerous. A man seized my collar and jerked me with great vigor out of the slot and onto my feet, on the platform. Moving to thank him I easily recognized Edwin Booth, having often seen him on the stage. I think that he later learned my name from a friend of his who was a fellow staff officer of mine, to whom I related the incident at City Point, in 1865."

President and Mrs. Lincoln, who had formed a warm friendship for Senator James Harlan and his wife, often invited them for long drives into the country. Senator Harlan says:

"During these drives to the country we had, of course, unrestrained conversation with each other,— very much, I think, as if we had been members of the same family.

"The last drive we had together occurred almost immediately after the fall of Richmond, and the surrender of the Confederates at Appomattox. On this occasion we four drove across the Potomac River, on Long Bridge into Virginia, and thence in the direction of Falls Church, through the country still marred and scarred—perhaps I ought to say *devastated*—by the recent presence of the great armies who had stripped it of almost every vestige of the environments of civilized life, including its once comfortable habitations, outbuildings, orchards, field fences, gardens and ornamental shrubbery. Even the hills had been deprived of their once majestic forests of native trees. After a long drive, occupying several hours, we returned to Washington to resume the drudgery of our respective official stations.

"This drive has become for me historical;—first, because it was the last one taken by me in his company and proved to have been so near the end of his life; and, secondly, because he had suddenly become, on the fall of Richmond and the surrender of the Confederate Army, April 9, at Appomattox, a different man. His whole appearance, poise, and bearing had marvelously changed. He was, in fact, transfigured. That indescribable sadness which had previously seemed to me an adamantine element of his very being had been suddenly changed for an equally indescribable expression of serene joy!—as if conscious that the great purpose of his life had been achieved. His countenance had become radiant,—emitting spiritual light something like a halo. Yet there was no manifestation of exaltation or ecstasy. He seemed the very personification of supreme satisfaction. His conversation was, of course, correspondingly exhilarating."

Besides the regular announcement of the play to be seen at Ford's Theatre, Friday night, April 14, a special notice had been inserted in "City Items" of the *Evening Star.*

"Ford's Theatre. Honor to our Soldiers! A new and patriotic song and chorus has been written by Mr. H. B. Phillips, and will be sung this evening by the Entire Company to do honor to Lieutenant General Grant and President Lincoln and Lady, who will visit the Theatre in compliment to Miss Laura Keene, whose benefit and last appearance is announced in the bills of the day. The music of the above song is composed by Professor W. Withers, Jr."

Harry Chapman Ford said that about half past eleven in the morning his father told Wilkes Booth of the coming visit of the President to the evening performance, and knowing Booth's sympathies for the South and also to tease him, mentioned that they would "have Jeff Davis and Bob Lee, handcuffed and shackled, in the opposite box." "My father," commented Mr. Ford, "always considered that this thoughtless jest hurried Booth to a quicker line of action."

Friday afternoon was cold, raw, and gusty. The sky was overcast with dark clouds, the air was penetrating and chilly with occasional showers.

The President and Mrs. Lincoln in spite of the very inclement weather went for their accustomed drive,

and Mrs. Lincoln asked if he would like to invite any
friends to drive with them. "No, I prefer to ride by
ourselves to-day," he answered. Mr. Lincoln was su-
premely happy now that the war had come to a close.
"We must be more cheerful in the future, Mary; between the war and the loss of our darling Willie we
have been very miserable."

Mr. Lincoln seemed so happy and cheerful that
Mary's heart was filled with joy. "I have not seen you
so happy since before Willie's death," she said to him.
"Mary," he replied, "we have had a hard time of it
since we came to Washington, but the war is over, and
with God's blessing we may hope for four years of
peace and happiness, and then we will go back to Illinois and pass the rest of our lives in quiet. We have
laid by some money, and during this term we will try
and save up more, but I shall not have enough to support us. We will go back to Illinois, and I will open
a law office at Springfield or Chicago and practice law
and at least do enough to help give us a livelihood."

It was late in the afternoon when they returned from
their drive. A group of friends, Richard Oglesby,
then governor of Illinois, among them, were crossing
the lawn towards the treasury. The President called
to them, "Come back, boys, come back." Mary Lincoln smiled tenderly and happily as she heard her

husband call these dignified, titled men "boys." Yes, after all, at heart, men were only boys. Remembering the fear-ridden gloomy months so recently passed, Mary marveled that to-day her spirit should be soaring with almost her old-time gayety, in spite, too, of a headache from which she had been suffering all day. They entered the White House—Mary went to her room to rest, leaving Mr. Lincoln and his friends laughing and jesting. Governor Oglesby said:

"Lincoln got to reading some humorous book—I think it was by 'John Phoenix.' They kept sending for him to come to dinner. He promised each time to go, but would continue reading the book. Finally he got a sort of peremptory order that he must come to dinner at once. It was explained to me by the old man at the door that they were going to have dinner and then go to the theater."

It was after eight o'clock when the Presidential theater party left the White House. The guests of honor for whom the party had been designed, General and Mrs. Grant, had left the city early in the evening, and, although Mrs. Lincoln was indisposed and the President who had seen the play once before was reluctant to go, they did not wish to disappoint the public, and inviting two young friends, Miss Harris and Major Rathbone, to go with them, ordered the carriage. It was late when the Presidential party drew up before Ford's Theater. As they made their way along the gallery behind the seats of the dress circle, the audience cheered, the orchestra played "Hail to the Chief," the actors in the meantime standing silent. The President's party passed into the box, laid aside their wraps, and bowing and smiling, seated themselves. The President occupied a large armchair at the left, Mrs. Lincoln next to him, Miss Harris next, and to the extreme right, Major Rathbone, a little behind Miss Harris.

The President was amused and laughed good-humoredly at the jokes in the play; he chatted courteously with his guests between the acts. It was draughty in the box. At a look from Mary, Mr. Lincoln rose from his seat and swung into his overcoat. He settled his long form back into the chair, all laughing happily. A shot! A moment's deadly silence—a woman's agonized scream—a cry of "Murder!" The audience, viewing a stage comedy, suddenly realized that a tragedy had been enacted in real life—then a pandemonium of excitement and fierce anger. Women fainted, men hoarsely screamed for vengeance against the assassin.

Mary Lincoln, with ashen cheeks and lips, her eyes wide with tragic horror and despairing grief, stood a moment with her hands pressed to her heart in the old familiar gesture of trying to still its tumultuous beating—then she sunk to her knees at the feet of her dying husband in a panic of uncontrollable grief. This threatened and awful calamity that she had feared so long, and that had destroyed her sense of happy security for four long years, had fallen at last like a thunderbolt out of a clear sky—just when she had come to think that the danger was past and that she and her husband had before them years of happiness and peace.

Major Rathbone attempted vainly to hold the assassin, who slashed him with a knife and, slashing and cutting all who stood in his way, escaped, for a time, with a broken leg. Miss Laura Keene went to the front of the stage and tried to calm the frantic audience. "For God's sake have presence of mind and keep your places, and all will be well." Miss Harris came to the front of the box and called, "Miss Keene, bring some water. Has anyone any stimulants?" "What is it? What is the matter?" Miss Keene inquired. "The President is shot," answered Miss Harris. Physicians were hurriedly called, the silent figure reclining so quietly and calmly in the armchair was stretched on the floor and the search for the wound was in progress when Miss Laura Keene reached the box. Miss Keene dropped to the floor and lifted the unconscious President's head in her arms, and her dress stained crimson from the wound in his head indicated the entrance of the fatal bullet.

The silent figure was tenderly lifted and carried out of the theater to the street. A helpless pause—and one of the bearers asked, "Where shall we take him?" A man was standing on the opposite side of the street wondering what could be the meaning of the excited crowds, seeing a grief-stricken woman with flowers in her hair and hearing someone say "The President is shot." Hearing the bearer ask, "Where shall we take him?" "Bring him here into my room," he said, coming quickly forward. The still unconscious form of the President was carried up the high steps and placed upon a hastily prepared bed in a small room in the house across the street from Ford's Theater. Surgeons and physicians gathered about the President in a desperate effort to save his life. Among the physicians was Dr. Beecher Todd of Lexington, Kentucky, a cousin and dear friend of Mrs. Lincoln.

Messengers were sent in every direction, one hastened to the White House to summon Robert Lincoln, who had only that day arrived in Washington. Intimate friends and prominent officials had quickly gathered. The death-like stillness was only broken by the labored breathing of the dying man and the heart-breaking sobs and moans of his wife, "Oh, my God, and must I give my husband to die?" she moaned in a voice of anguish. Captain Robert Lincoln, weeping bitterly, stood at the head of the bed by the side of Senator Sumner. The long night wore away. Mr. Robert Lincoln told the author he thought the interminable agony of this night would never end, the hopeless watching, the anguished weeping, finally, the utter, peaceful stillness of death—at twenty-two minutes after seven o'clock on Saturday morning. The bells all over Washington tolled for the death of the President. Houses and streets were hung with black, flags at half-mast—the crowds on the streets were white-faced and whispering.

The shock of this great culminating blow shattered the last of Mary Lincoln's reserve force already so weakened by former losses and repressions. Her collapse was utter and complete. She could not lift her head from the pillow without fainting. Little Tad never left her, his grief was so frantic that his mother tried to control herself to comfort Tad. Sunday morning the sun rose in brilliant splendor, and Tad took it to be a sign that his father was happy in heaven. "I am glad he has gone there," he exclaimed, "for he was never happy after he came here. This was not a good place for him."

WILLIAM WALLACE LINCOLN
Born December 21, 1850. Died
February 20, 1862. Photographed
about 1860

ROBERT TODD LINCOLN
About 1867

THOMAS LINCOLN (TAD)
From a photograph taken at the
White House about 1864

MARY TODD LINCOLN
Photograph taken in 1860

The bullet which took the life of her beloved husband practically ended the life of Mary Todd Lincoln. She was martyred by the same bullet and for the same cause which made Abraham Lincoln a deified martyr. Her husband's agony was soon over, stilled in peaceful death, while she, with this mortal wound in her heart, must linger and suffer untold agony for many years. She wrote afterwards, "All I wished then was to die, if it had been our Heavenly Father's will." (From letter to Congressman Orne.)

She and her son Robert were overwelmed by an avalanche of letters and telegrams. I am quoting three of particular interest, one from Queen Victoria, one from the Empress Eugenie, and one from Louis Philippe D'Orléans, better known as the Comte de Paris.

"Osborne.
April 29, 1865.

"Dear Madam,

Though a stranger to you I cannot remain silent when so terrible a calamity has fallen upon you and your country, and must personally express my *deep* and *heartfelt* sympathy with you under the shocking circumstances of your present dreadful misfortune.

No one can better *appreciate* than *I* can, who am myself *utterly brokenhearted* by the loss of my own beloved Husband, who was the light of my life,—my stay—*my all,—*

what your sufferings must be; and I earnestly pray that you may be supported by Him to whom alone the sorely stricken can look for comfort, in this hour of heavy affliction.

With renewed expressions of true sympathy, I remain dear Madam,

Your sincere friend

VICTORIA."

"Madame: L'Empereur fait parvenie à Washington les témoignages officials de l'indignation et de la douleur qu'inspire à la France le coup fatal vient de frapper le President Lincoln.

Mais a côté de cette calamité nationale il y a un malheur domestique qui éveillé dans mon cœur une emotion profond. Je veux, Madame, vous en offrir personnellement l'expression, ainsi que l'assurance des vœux que j'adresse au ciel pour qu'il vous donne la force de supporter cette cruelle épreuve. Croyez, Madame, à ma vive sympathie et à mos sentiments les plus sincères.

EUGENIE.

Paris 28 avril, 1865.
　Tuileries."

"York House,
Truckenham, S. W.
May 5th, 1865.

"Madam:
The overwhelming affliction which has befallen you and which has spread mourning not only over your country but

over the whole world, ought perhaps to command my silent sympathy.   But that national calamity is also a personal loss to me who had many opportunities of appreciating him-self the noble heart, the great qualities of M. Lincoln who held from him his commission in the Federal army and who gratefully remembers the gracious and friendly manner in which it was tendered to him.   I hope therefore that you will excuse the liberty I take to offer you the expression of my sincere condolence with your grief.   It is an impulse which I could not resist, an homage which I am anxious to pay to a great and respected memory.

Nobody pretends to offer you any consolations, for what mean the voices of the whole world when the only voice which we long to hear once more is silent forever?   But the expressions of sympathy are, perhaps, more acceptable when they come from one who has gone himself through the terrible ordeal of great and untimely family losses.

It is with those feelings that I beg you, Madam, to be-lieve me

Your most devoted,
Louis Philippe D'Orléans."

CHAPTER XII

AS SOON as Mary Lincoln and her son Robert were calm enough to think of themselves and their affairs, they settled all their debts in Washington—no one at the Capital should say that President Lincoln died insolvent. She, to be sure, had some personal debts which she must and would pay later if the New York merchants would give her time. She wrote to Congressman Orne:

"I told you what my eldest son and I have always kept to ourselves, that as soon as our senses could be regained I had every Washington and every other indebtedness sent to me and out of every dollar I could command I paid to the utmost farthing. In some cases known to the Administration, but in very few, it was all done by ourselves, my son and myself, out of our money, so it should be said President Lincoln was not in debt. This is one of the causes why I am so straitened now, for living as we were compelled to, my husband not being a rich man, and we had to pay enormous prices for everything those war times."

For five weeks after her husband's death Mary Lincoln had not been able to rise from her bed, and then came the heart-breaking task of packing up to leave the White House, each article had some association with her dear dead—Willie—her husband. Lizzie Keckley, the efficient colored seamstress, who had taken tender care of her during her five weeks' illness, superintended the packing, and in May, 1865, broken in health and mind, Mary Lincoln, accompanied by her two sons, Robert and Tad, left the White House for Chicago.

There was a long delay in the settlement of Mr. Lincoln's estate and by 1867 the $22,000 allotted her by Congress for the President's unfinished term had grown alarmingly less. The bills for unsettled accounts that she had asked the merchants to send her had come all too promptly and she was overwhelmed at their magnitude; mortified and terror stricken, too, at her inability to settle her indebtedness, she was dazed and did not know where to turn for help. For at this time Mary was a singularly lonely woman. Due to her mental trouble, which had been daily increasing ever since her husband's death, her former good judgment had become impaired. Her sisters and other relatives who voiced to Mary their indignant protests, entreating her to curb her excitement and eccentricity, only incurred her anger and had become estranged from her; they did not understand until later, the tragic cause which

finally several physicians and a jury of twelve men pronounced—insanity. These terrible debts were making
her head ache. She felt as if red-hot needles were being
driven through her brain. Honesty was ingrained in
Mary's code of life, and these merchants must not
suffer loss through her folly. She must sell everything!
It would be humiliating.

In her extremity and weakness she reverted to the
impulse of her childhood, which had been to seek the
love and help she had unfailingly found in her black
mammy who had shielded her from many a deserved
scolding. In the faithful, sympathetic colored woman,
Elizabeth Keckley, formerly a slave in a good old Virginia family, Mary saw the only available substitute,
and to her she turned blindly for sympathy and advice
—with most disastrous result. Mary, with the aid of
Elizabeth Keckley, attempted to dispose of laces,
frocks, everything—it was a dismal failure. Her piti-
ful efforts to settle her debts brought down upon her
head insults and vituperation from the press both
North and South. No one seemed to recognize the
sturdy honesty which made this shrinking woman willing to swallow her pride in this futile adventure. She
was frantic with humiliation at the publicity and criti-
cisms; her heavy black crêpe veil was drawn closer
and more and more did she shrink from an unsympa-

thetic, misunderstanding world. Nor did she suffer alone, as the following will show.

Extract from letter written to Miss Mary Harlan by Robert Todd Lincoln:

Oct. 16th, '67

Chicago, Illinois

"I suppose you have seen some of the papers so there is no need of detailing what I was told they were full of. I did not read them. The simple truth, which I cannot tell to anyone not personally interested, is that my mother is on one subject not mentally responsible. I have suspected this for some time from various indications and now have no doubt of it. I have taken the advice of one or two of my friends in whom I trust most and they tell me I can do nothing. It is terribly irksome to sit still under all that has happened and say nothing, but it has to be done. The greatest misery of all is the fear of what may happen in the future. This is, of course, not to be foreseen and is what troubles me most. I have no doubt that a great many good and amiable people wonder why I do not take charge of her affairs and keep them straight but it is very hard to deal with one who is sane on all subjects but one. You could hardly believe it possible, but my mother protests to me that she is in actual want and nothing I can do or say will convince her to the contrary. Do you see that I am likely to have a good deal of trouble in the future, do what I can to prevent it."

Mary Lincoln was not the only one in that fatal box at Ford's Theater, April 14, 1865, whose reason was dethroned by shock. Poor Major Rathbone, years later, was adjudged insane and his experience on that tragic night was supposed to have been the cause.

There were intervals, however, when Mary was almost her brave, normal, high-spirited self and a stranger meeting her would see no trace of an unbalanced mentality. At other times, with her brain on fire with pain, she was submerged in gloom and her heart was filled with bitterness against the sad fate which had overtaken her. At such times—sunk in despair, inert, listless, no courage left to fight the battle of life—she ironically contrasted her situation with that of those who were winning the plaudits of a grateful North and were being showered with magnificent gifts of houses and bank accounts while she, the widow of the murdered chief, was overwhelmed with unkindness. When Charles Sumner, that staunch friend of her husband and herself, urged Congress to make her an appropriation, Congress hesitated long years over an appropriation of twenty-five thousand dollars and an annuity of two thousand dollars—both were finally granted before her death but with so much reluctance,

DAVID TODD, MARY TODD LINCOLN'S HALF BROTHER
From a photograph taken about 1862

Mrs. Charles Kellogg (Margaret Todd), the Eldest of Mrs. Lincoln's
Half Sisters

wrangling, and rudeness that any graciousness attached
to the nation's gift was lost in the manner of its be-
stowal. "Rich gifts wax poor, when the giver proves
unkind."

The image of her husband filled Mary's heart and
mind. The past—there was no past for her in which
he did not figure; the present was overflowing with
horror at his tragic death; the future loomed a dreary
interminable waste without his dear companionship.
Broken-hearted, bewildered, she was like a traveler
lost in the desert. She did not know where to turn,
where to find an oasis of comfort. She hungered and
thirsted for sympathy and friendship. Restless and
unhappy, she wandered from one lonely spot to another
seeking what she could never hope to find, peace,
health, surcease from her overwhelming sorrow. Pur-
sued by ignorant gossip, she became extremely sensitive
and avoided notoriety by living in the most unostenta-
tious, quiet way possible. While her husband lived
she could smile and jest at the unpleasant things said
of them both; but now her smiles were tears, her jests
were sobs. She was truly a victim of the cruel times
in which she lived, a suffering, innocent creature,
whose only crime was her prominence.

Mrs. Shipman writes that sometime in the latter part
of the sixties she was visiting in Chicago. Just before

she left Louisville, Kentucky, she promised Mr. and
Mrs. Speed that she would call on Mrs. Lincoln who
was then in Chicago. Mrs. Shipman, though somewhat impressed by the newspaper stories of Mrs. Lincoln and advised by the friends she was visiting that
Mrs. Lincoln lived in strictest seclusion and declined
to receive or to return any calls, was discouraged but
at the same time resolved to fulfill her promise. To
her surprise Mrs. Lincoln not only received her cordially but returned her call the next day. This meeting with the daughter of one of Mrs. Lincoln's intimate girlhood friends developed into a warm friendship.

Mrs. Shipman relates an incident that happened
when she and her brother were in Baltimore at Bar-
num's Hotel. Mrs. Lincoln was there at the same time
with Robert and Tad. The two latter having to return
to Washington, Mrs. Lincoln asked Mrs. Shipman and
her brother to accompany her in to dinner. As they
entered the dining room they heard on all sides, from
whispers to loud tones, "Mrs. Lincoln, Mrs. Lincoln."
"Some of the guests," said Mrs. Shipman, "so far for-
getting themselves as to rise from their seats to stare at
her. Mrs. Lincoln was embarrassed and indignant,
and this was a mild exhibition of the vulgar imperti-
nence to which she was habitually exposed on her

travels. It has been said, perhaps untruthfully, that she sometimes traveled incognito. If she did, is it any wonder that having the courage of a strong individuality she tried to escape this ill-bred vulgar curiosity by so simple a stratagem?"

To quote Mrs. Shipman again:

"My opportunities for judging her entitle me to speak of her [Mrs. Lincoln] with some confidence. In her younger days she was intimate with my mother and in later years during the trying period of her widowhood I saw a great deal of her under a variety of circumstances. She was vivacious and mercurial, full of repartee and dash but never unrefined; and though by nature light-hearted was never light-headed. Her conversation and letters plainly betokened the cultivated lady. She was perfectly frank and extremely high-spirited and, when she thought the occasion demanded it, capable no doubt of a cutting expression. A more affectionate heart I never knew. In mental training, intelligence, and accomplishments, quite equal to her position and more than the equal of many of those who have occupied it. She bore herself throughout as a warm-hearted, whole-souled, high-spirited Kentucky woman, which she was."

"No woman," wrote another friend of Mrs. Lincoln's, "ever sustained the dignity of widowhood with more appropriate behavior. Only once did she lay aside her heavy weeds, and this at the earnest solicitation of her son Tad on the occasion of his birthday, when she wore a plain black silk dress, but never again could she be induced to put off her deep mourning which was the external emblem of her incurable grief."

Mr. Paul Shipman writes to the editor of the Louisville *Courier-Journal:*

"General Badeau in the New York *World* gives his personal recollections of Mrs. Lincoln. 'While I was Consul General at London,' he says, 'I learned of her [Mrs. Lincoln] living in an obscure quarter and went to see her. She was touched by the attention and when I asked her to my house—for it seemed wrong that the widow of the man who had done so much for us all should be ignored by an American representative—she wrote me a note of thanks, betraying how rare such courtesies had become to her then.' This is a little too much! If I ever catch the spirit of Mr. Toodles, I should make General Badeau's acquaintance and he should do me the honor to ask me to his house and I should accept or decline *without thanks*. I wish him to understand in advance that I omit the thanks simply and purely to exclude his conclusion that such courtesies have become rare with me. In the face of social

logic of this sort, a gentleman must needs show himself
a boor to prove himself not a beggar.   General Badeau
says Mrs. Lincoln was touched by the attention he paid
in calling on her.

"If thus easily touched, her sensibilities during her
short stay in London must have been rather heavily
taxed for I seldom met her that she did not have something to tell me of this, that or the other distinguished
person who had just called on her—now Bishop Simpson, now Mr. Motley, the Comte de Paris, and so on
to the end of the shining chapter.   General Badeau,
misled by his peculiar logic of etiquette, mistook her
civility as he misplaced his compassion.   Her polite-
ness he may rest assured was no appeal to his pity.   She
did not appear to think herself neglected.   But if
touched by his attention, I have no doubt she would
be touched, if living, by the apology he makes now for
having shown it.   She is dead, but the American people, it is to be hoped, will accept this apology.

"As to the quarter of London in which Mrs. Lincoln
lived, a word will suffice.   Her residence was in sight
of Bedford Square, perhaps five minutes' walk from
the British Museum, a quarter of London abounding
in noble mansions which throughout the first quarter
of this century held the rank and fashion of the town
and still holds the flower of its gentry.   It is an airy

sunny cheerful district of the metropolis, respectable in every sense and 'obscure' in none. Mrs. Lincoln, in fact, could scarcely have chosen a more suitable quarter. Her life at this time was subservient to Tad who lived with her, pursuing his studies under a tutor. She appeared wrapped up in him, shunned rather than courted attention and desired above all things peace and retirement.

"I saw a good deal of her, as my wife, of whom she was an old friend, could not go out at the time, she was often at our rooms and once I accompanied her to hear Spurgeon preach. I found her sympathetic, cordial, sensible, intelligent, and brimming with that bonhomie so fascinating in the women of your own South, of whom indeed she was one. No trace of eccentricity appeared in her conduct or manners. She was simply a bright, wholesome, attractive woman. I could not for the life of me recognize the Mrs. Lincoln of the newspapers in the Mrs. Lincoln I saw."

Mrs. Lincoln's eldest son, Robert Todd Lincoln, was a great stay and comfort to his mother. In 1868 he married Miss Mary Harlan, a very popular girl of Washington society. Mrs. Lincoln was delighted with her son's choice. Several years before President Lincoln's death, he had said to Mr. Stanton: "Mary is tremendously in love with Senator Harlan's little daughter. I think she has picked her out for a daughter-in-law. As usual, I think Mary has shown fine taste."

The first child of this marriage was named for her grandmother, Mary Todd Lincoln, and when Mrs. Shipman met Mrs. Abraham Lincoln in London, she says Mrs. Lincoln often spoke of her son Robert and his little family and was always planning to send them some gift. She sent her daughter-in-law a wrap of "silver gray and Marie Louise blue" and wrote her, "It is as pretty as can be and Bob will surely think you are more charming than ever when you are arranged in it." She finishes this: "I feel miserably blue to-day. I am just recovering from a severe attack of neuralgia in my head, accompanied by great indisposition which has been my faithful companion for more than two weeks—my health has been quite as bad as it was last winter. I am well aware without my physician so frequently repeating to me—that quiet is necessary to my life; therefore in such places, I must at present abide—certainly ill luck presided at my birth—certainly within the last few years it has been a faithful attendant."

Letter to Mrs. Orne:

"Frankfurt, February 11, 1869.

"Tomorrow is the anniversary of my dear husband's birthday and it may be, if my health continues to fail me as it is now so fast doing, another birthday will find me with him. I too, dear, loved Mr. Stanton yet he died peacefully on his bed almost five years after the close of the War. My husband, great, good, and glorious beyond all words of praise, was cruelly murdered, snatched from the side of the wife and family who adored him without being able to sigh a farewell."

Tad was a splendid manly fellow, and his mother completely submerged her life in his. Her supreme interest now was his education. She writes to Mrs. Orne from Frankfurt, Germany, December 29, 1869, "Taddie is like some old woman with regard to his care of me. His dark, loving eyes watching over me remind me so much of his dearly beloved father's."

Another letter to Mrs. Orne:

"If my darling husband had lived out his four years he promised me we should live our remaining years in a home we both should have enjoyed. * * * Bowed down and broken-hearted in my terrible bereavement my thoughts this last sad summer have often turned to you. I have remembered with most grateful emotions your tender sympathy in the first days of my overwhelming anguish. Time does not reconcile me to the loss of the most devoted and loving husband a sadly afflicted woman ever possessed. How

ALEXANDER H. TODD
The youngest of the Todd children, killed during a skirmish at
Baton Rouge, Louisiana, August, 1863

MRS. BEN HARDIN HELM (EMILIE TODD)
From a photograph made in 1864

dearly I long, my kind friend, to lay my aching head and sorrowing heart by the side of this dearly beloved one. When the summons comes for my departure I will gladly welcome it for there the weary are at rest."

It was her greatest pleasure to receive and answer letters from home. Few days passed that she did not write to her daughter-in-law.

"London
No. 9 Woburn Place
Russell Square.

"My dear Mary—your most acceptable letter was received to-day. Need I say to you, how much delight it affords me to hear from you. That blessed baby, how dearly I would love to look upon her sweet young face. If my boy Taddie and myself are wanderers in a strange land, our thoughts are continually with you and we speak of you very frequently—I have just received a letter from Mrs. Simpson who is now en route to Italy. When she left here we came to some understanding that I might join her about Christmas, in Rome. As a matter of course, even if it suited pecuniarily, which it does not, it would never do to have Taddie or his tutor accompany me. Taddie is closeted with his tutor seven and a half hours each day, and from Saturday to Saturday. When I am with him for three hours to listen to his examination of his studies of the week I can see a great improvement in him. But of course if I go to Italy the tutor must be relinquished and he placed in school or I must trust him to the stormy waves and the merciful Providence of our great Father in Heaven for safety and protection until he lands in America! Driving down to the bank at noon to-day for letters I proposed to Tad with a trembling voice and aching heart you may be sure, that he would embark on the *Russia* which sails next Saturday week for the U. S. Dec. 10th and go home pass his Christmas with you and Bob and immediately afterwards be placed in school. Study more than he does now he could not possibly do. If he only had the information of his tutor, who is most indefatigable, I told him to-day, I would be willing to live on a crust of bread a day —*almost*. To-night, we are engaged to meet Governor Evans and family and I am going to ask Governor Evans' candid advice on the subject. He came over last week on the same vessel. To trust my beautiful, darling *good* boy to the elements, at this season of the year, makes my heart faint within me. Each breath I drew would be a prayer for his safety, which only those who have been as deeply bereaved as myself could fully understand. On the other hand, the English schools have vacation for a month after Christmas which if I did not send Tad home would delay my going to Italy until the 1st of Feb., keeping him with his tutor in the mean-time at hard study.

I am troubled to hear of your dear mother's continued ill health. I do so trust that Bob will come over with you if it is only for three months, it would do him such a world of good. He loves you so *very dearly* and misses you very greatly. I was such an excessively indulged wife—my darling husband was so gentle and easy. You know you will always be FIRST LOVE of daughters-in-law. I often tell Tad I can scarcely flatter myself he will ever marry to suit me quite as well as dear Bob has done. Please present my warmest love to your mother and father. * * *"

"Florence, Italy—Feb. 12, 1870.

My dear Mary:

My servant woman and I have arrived safely after much fatigue in this beautiful Florence. We came through the charming Tyrol, via Milan and Lake Como, had a day's sail on the latter the beauties of which are simply *indescribable*. Passed three days at Geneva and found Mrs. Simpson and Ida here wondering what had become of me. Yesterday we went together to the Pitti Palace where the King resides and saw the room where the beautiful Princess Marguerite sleeps. We can only wish *her* health and happiness *all her days* knowing full well by experience that power and high position do not ensure a *bed of roses*. Mrs. S. has been here already four weeks. * * * Armed with my guide book, a desire to see all that is wonderful and strange and with my faithful domestic following in my wake, I must pursue my journey alone. At Venice, where Mrs. Simpson has not yet been, in three weeks' time we will meet and wend our way up to dear old Frankfurt, thence to England. I received a letter this morning from dear Tad, I wrote you that until the middle of April next he is placed with young Evans in an English school. I am neglecting to tell you that we visited the studio on yesterday of the man to whom the commission was given for the statue of my dearly beloved husband."—[Larkin Meade, the Sculptor].

"Frankfurt—March 22.

"My very dear Mary:

After a most tedious journey from Nice of constant travel for three days, I arrived here this morning. Of course, I sent immediately for my Taddie and as he has just left me for an hour, I feel that I cannot refrain from writing you, for your most welcome letter of March 1st has just been read. It pains me beyond expression, to learn of your recent illness and I deeply deplore that I was not with you to wait upon you. My dear child, do take good care of your precious health—*even the thought* of you at this great distance is a great alleviation to the sorrow I am enduring.

I may quietly return to you, as it is, nothing can please me in what is beyond doubt most necessary at the present time both to my health and to my peace of mind—this change of scene. My thoughts have been constantly with you for months past, and, oh! how I have wished day by day, that you could be with me and enjoy the air and the sunshine of the lovely climate I have just left. It would have been utterly impossible for me with my present health and sad state of mind, to have taken the least interest in Italian cities this winter. I return to find my dear boy much grown in even so short a time and I am pained to see his face thinner, although he retains his usual bright complexion. He is doubtless greatly improving in his studies, yet I am very sure the food he gets at his school does not agree with him. This you may be sure is a most painful belief to me. When I am here, I can always give him his dinner as he has their permission to be absent. His presence has become so necessary even to my life. In two days' time he will have his Easter vacation for ten days and he is urging me to take him *somewhere* at that time and if I were not so fatigued would gladly consent to do so, but I suppose it will end in my acquiescence with his wishes. * * *

Do oblige me by considering me as a mother for you are very dear to me as a daughter. *Anything* and *everything* is yours—if you will consider them worth an acceptance. My mind was so distracted with my grief in that house, 375, I cannot remember where anything was put. It will be such a relief to me to know that articles can be used and enjoyed by you. * * * Remember everything is yours and feeling so fully assured as you must be of my love, will you not, my dear girl, consider them as such? Oh! that I could be with you! for with the lonely life I impose upon myself, separation from those I love so much, at this trying, heart-rending time, is excruciating pain. If when we meet I find you restored to health I will feel in a measure compensated for the dreary absence. I am glad you enjoyed your visit to Springfield. They are all so pleasantly situated—so hospitable and so fully prepared to receive you with the greatest affection. Do make the promised visit to Mrs. Edwards—[Elizabeth Todd, Mrs. Lincoln's sister] in the summer and then go to the seaside and rest quietly for a month, no less time. Let me beseech you, dear Mary, to take care of your health.

My head aches now for the tears I have shed this morning in thinking of you and our loving boy. Taddie with his great good heart loves you so devotedly. I shall try to think of you as with your dear mother while it is so cold in Chicago at present. I know they will be careful of you. I never see anything particularly pretty—that I do not wish it was yours. My spirit is very willing but my purse not very extensive.

I am pained to hear of Bettie Stuart's death. She was a most amiable woman, and her father is a very dearly loved cousin—a most affectionate relative. Did you see Mrs. Lizzie Brown in Springfield?—a very sweet woman. I shall, dear Mary, await most anxiously news from you. If I do not hear soon I shall imagine every trouble. If you will write to dear Taddie, you will gratify him very much.

Referring to that speech Mrs. —— made you last winter that housekeeping and babies were an uncomfortable state of existence for a young married lady I think her experience was different from most mothers who consider that in the outset in life—a nice home—loving husband and precious child are the happiest stages of life. I fear she has grown moody, but at the same time I hope you will have a good rest and enjoy yourself *free* for a year or more to come. The Doctor has just left me and says he wonders to find me sitting up.

You should go out *every day* and enjoy yourself—you

are so *very young* and should be as gay as a lark. Trouble comes soon enough, my dear child, and you must enjoy life, whenever you can. We all love you so very much—and you are blessed with a devoted husband and darling child— *so do go out* and enjoy the sunshine. I do so hope your dear mother has recovered her health. When I can I will write to her. Do, I pray you, write frequently. I do wish you would take out the double India shawl, with a red center, which I never wore and make faithful use of it."

"Obennsel, Germany,
May 19th, 1870.

"My dear Mary:

I have come out here to pass a day or two with Taddie (his new school quarters) as I leave most probably tomorrow for Bohemia—a journey which will require fully twenty hours to accomplish. The first evening I will stop at the very old town of Nuremburg, so full of interest and perhaps remain there a day to see the old castles and churches. This morning in this old village five minutes by rail from Hamburg, I entered an old church with dates of 1610 on it. The Christs that are suspended on the walks around the town—bear dates 1704—until we get accustomed to seeing these things they appear very strange to *fresh American* eyes. When I came out here two or three days since, I had just returned from a most charming trip in the Odenwald Mountains, where the scenery is very beautiful also Tad went with me to Heidelburg, to Baden for a few hours and travelled in the *Black Forest*. At Heidelburg we ascended the mountain one morning about nine o'clock roamed through the ruins of the magnificent old castle and took our breakfast in the grounds where there is a very fine restaurant. At noon we proceeded to Baden and ascended another mountain height, in the evening to visit the ruins of another grand old castle—centuries back. The next day we went out to "La Favorita" the abode of the "White Lady." Taddie and I were continually wishing that you and Bob and that precious baby were with us.

Mrs. Lincoln writes to Mrs. Shipman:

"Frankfurt am Main,
June 29, 1870.

"My dear Mrs. Shipman:

Although weary months have passed since your very kind and welcome letter was received, yet notwithstanding it has so long remained unanswered. You have been very frequently in my thoughts and I have been mentally wishing you such a world of happiness in your new marriage relations. Your letter in the early spring found me quite an invalid and I have just returned from a long visit to the Marienbad baths and waters in Bohemia and I find my health greatly benefited. I can well imagine how greatly you have enjoyed your journeyings in Europe and I truly hope we may meet whilst we are both abroad. You with your life so filled with love and happiness, whilst I alas am but a weary exile. Without my beloved husband's presence, the world is filled with gloom and dreariness for me.

I am going with my young son in a day or two into the country to remain some weeks. If you will kindly write me and direct to care of Philip Nicoll Schmidt, Bankers, Frankfurt, Am Main, Germany, I will receive it. The name of the gentleman you have married is too prominent a one in America not to be familiar to me and associated with one so highly gifted as Mr. Prentice was. The gems of poetry he has written will always fill our minds and hearts with remembrance of him. Dickens too has passed away. How much delight it would give me to meet you this summer. Do you ever hear from our amiable and lovely friend, Mrs. Speed? With compliments to Mr. Shipman and many affectionate congratulations to yourself.

I remain always truly yours,
MARY LINCOLN."

She writes to Mrs. Orne:

"Frankfurt, Germany,
August 17, 1870.

"I must speak of my young boy. He has become so homesick and at the same time his English education has become so neglected that I have consented with many a heartache to permit him to go home."

With her heart quivering and aching, she had ever before her the image of her idolized husband. Travel could not dim her grief, and she dreaded a return to America, where her memories would be quickened into more vivid pain.

"August 20

"Dear Mary. My very pleasant and affectionate friend arrived in town since I wrote the first part of this letter—Mrs. Orne. She came from Hamburg in search of me and has rooms at the same Hotel where I am now stopping. We are together all the time. She is a very lovely woman and will remain here some time, she says, to be with me. I feel quite made up."

This note was slipped into a sad letter which Mrs. Lincoln had just written her daughter-in-law. The joy she expresses in the love and companionship of her friend—Mrs. Orne, shows how lonely she had been, how she craved understanding and friendship—but nothing, for long, could still that urge for constant change of scene which drove her from place to place in the vain effort to drown thought and sorrow.

"Leamington, England,
Sept. 10, 1870.

"My dear Mary,

Your very welcome letter was received last evening. Taddie and his tutor began their studies together on yesterday, both appear deeply interested. He comes to us most highly recommended, and I shall see that not a moment will be idly passed. From eight until one o'clock each day Tad is seated at his table—with his tutor studying and from five to seven each evening with his tutor he is studying his lessons. On no occasion do I intend that he shall deviate from this rule. I have just been in to see him studying, and they are earnestly engaged—for dear life. The gentleman who is teaching him is very highly educated—very quiet and gentlemanly and patience itself. Tad now realizes the great necessity of an education, and I am sure will do well. I am coughing so badly that I can scarcely write. I left Liverpool last Saturday afternoon so completely sick that I determined to come on here to be well attended to. This is the first day I have sat up since then and a physician tells me that as soon as possible I should go to a dryer climate. It will be a great trial to separate myself from dear Mrs. Orne who has proved so loving a friend to me. But my health is again beginning to fail me as it did last winter. I can only hope that I can secure some quiet Southern nook to rest—until the disturbances in Italy have ceased. When I see you I can tell you a great deal about the war which I cannot now write.

Later in October she writes again:

"Leamington, England,
October 27, '70.

"My dear Mrs. Shipman:

Your very kind and welcome letter of September 27 has just been received from Frankfurt. I cannot express to you how deeply I regret not being in Frankfurt when you were there. I have been absent most of the time from Germany since last June, have been occasionally in London but this I have considered my resting place. I am exceedingly anxious to meet you, and if you could not come here to the loveliest garden spot of Europe I would run up any time to London. In three hours and a half we arrive there passing through Oxford. Very possibly you may have been here,—surrounded by Kenilworth Castle, Warwick Castle, Stratford-on-Avon, nine miles distant, and only a very pleasant drive. My son of course is here with me. I have been fortunate enough to secure a very fine English tutor for him, who comes to us very highly recommended, a very fine scholar and a gentlemanly, conscientious man. He recites his lessons with his tutor seven hours of each day, so you can imagine that I see very little of my dear, good son. If he improves as he is doing I shall be satisfied. Many Americans are always here. One especial family with whom I have been very intimate for years, has been with me all the time. Again I repeat, I long to see you. My remembrance of you is of a very agreeable nature, and in this strange land those whom we have formerly loved become doubly dear. Hoping that I may soon hear from you, my dear friend, and with compliments for your husband and much love for yourself.

Your affectionate friend,
MARY LINCOLN."

"9 Woburn Place,
Russell Square, Jan. 13, 1871.

"My dear Mrs. Shipman:

I have concluded in the weakness of my *Mother* heart to accompany my son out to his school and perhaps remain a

day or two near him.   As the movement is somewhat unexpected, I have in consequence not a moment to lose and it
grieves me to say not even an opportunity of saying to you,
for whom I entertain so true and firm a friendship, farewell.   Even now I am being hurried, yet I could not leave
your neighborhood without committing my regrets to paper.
I shall hope soon to hear the good news that your health
has improved.   I go myself coughing most disagreeably
and a bundle of wrappings.   My servant woman has proved
herself within the past week a good nurse.   With kind regards to Mr. Shipman and ever so much love to your dear
self, believe me always

Your truly affectionate friend,
Mary Lincoln."

"London, January 26th, 1871.

"My dear Mary

Count de Paris came in about a week since, twelve miles
from Tuckenham, to see me, having only heard the day
before that I was in town.   He then wished me to name a
day when I would drive with them, and on my table this
morning I find a most urgent note to come out to visit them.
I will do so, on my return in the spring. * * *

Be sure to write often to me for everything connected
with you or yours is of *deep, deep* interest to me.   How
pained I am, dear Mary, to hear of your beloved mother's
continued illness.   Tad is often very anxious to hear of
your brother for he, with his loving heart, is very much
attached to him.   Tad is almost wild to see Bob, you and

the baby; he thinks the latter must be a rare young lady, I am also of his opinion. I scarcely imgained when I began this letter that my strength would hold out for more than three pages, but the themes which we discuss together in our epistles are decidedly exciting and exhaustless. * * *"

When homesickness at last became unendurable to both Tad and his mother, they returned to America and were welcomed in the home of her son Robert T. Lincoln and his wife in Chicago.

In May, 1871, Mrs. Abraham Lincoln wrote to her cousin Eliza Stuart:

> "Wabash Avenue,
> May ——.

"My dear Cousin:

My young son is confined to his bed with a severe cold and in consequence we will not remove to the Clifton House until Saturday. We are received with so much affection here and notwithstanding the confined limits of this charming little home my son Robert, who is all that is noble and good and his lovely little wife will not hear to our removal. Yet as she is compelled to go instantly to her mother, who is in a most critical state, I think we had best make the change. In reality when they return, of course we will be almost always together. I love my son's wife whom I have known since she was a child just as well as my own sons and her warm heart has always been mine. You are so amiable and good and will appreciate all such kindly relations. Dear Cousin Eliza, when you are coming in town with Lizzie drop in and see me. Broken-hearted as I am over my deep bereavement, yet the memory of earlier years and the memory of those who were so kind to me in my desolate childhood is ever remembered by me. My life was so enriched by the most loving and devoted of husbands which makes the present all the more sorrowful to bear. Do come. I trust you will remain in town some days longer.

With much love I remain,

Your affectionate cousin,
MARY LINCOLN."

To Mary Lincoln's clouded mind and abysmal sorrow, even her happy, carefree, tomboy childhood, filled with more than the usual luxuries and advantages, seemed desolate without the presence of her beloved husband. Only the life she spent with him seemed worth while and happy—that part of the past without him seemed desolate, and though she had two loving and devoted sons and a daughter-in-law as dear to her as her own sons, the present without her "most loving and devoted husband" was too sorrowful to bear.

Tad was well enough to be moved to the Clifton House but soon after grew much worse.

"Mt. Pleasant, Iowa,
July 3rd, 1871.

"Dear Robert:

I received yours of the 25th and 28th on my return home after a week's absence in the interior of the State. I was wretchedly uneasy about your Brother, and could hear nothing: telegraphed from Davenport on Friday, but received no reply. I infer from all the intimations from Washington and your silence that he must be better—and I trust out of danger. I am very solicitous to have Mary with her Mother as much as possible while I am compelled to be absent: it is almost a necessity that this should be so, or that I should give up the contest here, as every imaginable scheme is being resorted to to control the election of Members of the "general assembly." As I am in it, perhaps it would be as well for you and Willie that I should go successfully through, if I can do so honorably. But this requires my presence in the State for the time being. And yet I would not remain away from Mrs. Harlan unless assured that she is both well taken care of and satisfied. When Mary is with her I know everything will be right. But I feel that this imposes a hardship on you, which perhaps ought not to be permitted.

Page 2, Senator Harlan's letter:

I wish you would send me the paper announcing Allison's arrival as "U. S. Senator from Iowa."

Yours truly,
Jas. Harlan.

"Since writing the foregoing I have received a telegram via Muscatine.

J. H.

"R. T. Lincoln, Esq.,
Chicago, Ill.

Extracts from letter written by Robert Todd Lincoln to his wife:

"Chicago, July 11, 1871.
"* * * Mr. Thomas Lincoln has been picking up for the last two or three days and is to all appearances improving, his face has lost some of its expression of distress.* * *"

Tad seemed to be improving and Robert Lincoln and his mother were so relieved they could smile and jest with the beginning of hope that "Mr. Thomas Lincoln" would recover, but three days later, July 14, in another letter to his wife, Robert Lincoln says:

"I am sorry to tell you that Tad seems to be losing ground. Yesterday was very hot and oppressive and he got in a bad way during the night and this morning was nearly as bad as the first night you came to the Clifton House. I have just now (2 o'clock) come from him and he is looking and feeling better, but Dr. Davis says he can see nothing to found any hope of his recovery upon and that he can live only a few days—with the weak action of his heart and lungs. To-day there is a fine breeze and the air is really delightful—all of which makes him feel better but really have little or no effect upon his trouble. He is looking dreadfully."

The next day, July 15, Tad breathed his last.

Extracts from letter to Mrs. Robert Lincoln from her husband:

"We came back from Springfield this morning all well. I will not attempt to tell you all that has happened in the last ten days, for I am a good deal used up. Last Tuesday, Wednesday and Thursday morning Tad appeared a great deal better. He was stronger and looking well and the water was reduced a good deal in his chest. Thursday was very close and oppressive and it pulled him back very much. Friday afternoon he seemed to rally again and at eleven P. M. was sleeping nicely with prospects of having a good night, so I left him with mother and his two nurses and went to the house. I was aroused at half past four and went to the hotel and saw at once that he was failing fast. He was in great distress and laboring for breath and ease but I do not think he was in acute pain. He lingered on so until between half past seven and eight, when he suddenly threw himself forward on his bar and was gone. Poor mother was almost distracted but Mrs. —— devoted herself to her, and we took her up to the house. During the day Mrs. ——, Mrs. Farlin and Mrs. Wm. H. Brown were with her. The next morning Mrs. Dr. Brown and your father came. We had services in the house in the afternoon and at night I went down to Springfield—with a car full of friends. Mother was utterly exhausted and could not go but Mrs. Dr. Brown stayed with her until I got back. I have a nurse with her and she is doing very well—better than I expected. I hope and expect that in a few days I will get her to go down to Springfield to my aunt Mrs. Edwards, and if so I will think I have done a good deal.

"I am very glad the picture of the baby [Mary Todd Lincoln, named for her grandmother] came in Friday for Tad was delighted with it and it was really the last pleasure he had on earth."

His poor mother, frantic with anxiety, had nursed Tad without rest or sleep until the end—and with his death a crushing weight was added to her burden of sorrow and denser clouds to her already clouded mentality.

Four years later, May 19, 1875, her son Robert, with the deepest grief, was compelled to have her placed in a sanitarium. The following letters will explain themselves.

"Chicago,
June 1, 1875.

"Mrs. J. H. Orne.
My dear Madam:

Your letter written immediately after you received the news of the proceedings which I was unhappily compelled to take, should have received an earlier reply and I must beg you to excuse my apparent neglect. If you have since then seen any detailed account of the occurrences which forced me to place my mother under care, I think, indeed, know, you could not but have approved my action. Six physicians in council informed me that by longer delay I was making myself morally responsible for some very probable tragedy, which might occur at any moment. Some of my Eastern friends have criticized the public proceedings in court, which seemed to them unnecessary. Against this there was no help, for we have a statute in this State which imposes a very heavy penalty on any one depriving an insane person of his liberty without the verdict of a jury. My mother is, I think, under as good care and as happily situated as is possible under the circumstances. She is in the private part of the house of Dr. Patterson and her associates are the members of his family only. With them she walks and drives whenever she likes and takes her meals with them or in her own room as she chooses, and she tells me she likes them all very much. The expression of surprise at my action which was telegraphed East, and which you doubtless saw, was the first and last expression of the kind she has uttered and we are on the best of terms. Indeed my consolation in this sad affair is in thinking that she herself is happier in every way, in her freedom from care and excitement, than she has been in ten years. So far as I can see she does not realize her situation at all. It is of course my care that she should have everything for her comfort and pleasure that can be obtained. I can tell you nothing as to the probability of her restoration. It must be the work of some time if it occurs. Her physician who is of high repute is not yet able to give an opinion. The responsibility that has been and is now on me is one that I would gladly share if it was possible to do so, but being alone as I am, I can only do my duty as it is given me to see it. Trusting that I am guided for the best.

Very sincerely yours,

ROBERT T. LINCOLN."

"August 8th.

"Robert T. Lincoln, Esq.,
Dear Sir:

Your letter dated June 1st has just reached me on my return from Saratoga. I thank you very much for it. It is a great comfort to hear from your own self, of the loving care and wise guidance which your dear Mother is under. Not that I ever had one doubt of that, for I know too much of your goodness as a son from her own lips to ever allow the first thought or suggestion to have any influence over me, and I doubt if there ever was more than one or two persons that had, for at Saratoga where there is always a great concourse of people, I never heard the first person say ought but that you had done perfectly right and spoke warmly in your praise also. I only wish all the States had the same "Statute." It is a blessed one. I can readily see how comfortable your dear Mother is made by your thoughtful care, and can with you believe her happier than she has been for years. Dear precious one! How my heart goes out towards her in love and affection! You may hope for her restoration. The physicians both here and in Europe pronounced my son-in-law incurable. Still he surprised them all with return to health. There is a "Great Physician" above all others "whose arm is not shortened" and to whom we may all look. God give you strength to bear up under this chastening, and crown your days with such happiness that such a son of such a father most justly deserves. And now, Mr. Lincoln, if there is ever anything I can do for your Mother, remember I am at your service.

With kind regards to yourself and your wife, I remain with great respect,

Yours very truly,

SALLY B. ORNE."

At the end of eleven months Mary Lincoln was declared sane. Her sister Elizabeth (Mrs. Edwards) went to the sanitarium at Batavia and, accompanied by her sister and a trained nurse, Mary went back to Springfield. She was depressed and unhappy. "I cannot endure to meet my former friends, Lizzie," she said bitterly; "they will never cease to regard me as a lunatic, I feel it in their soothing manner. If I should say the moon is made of green cheese they would heartily and smilingly agree with me. I love you, but I cannot stay. I would be much less unhappy in the midst of strangers."

Mrs. Edwards, knowing that her sister was far from normal, felt very apprehensive to see her leave but she put no obstacle in her way; indeed, she came to think that a complete change might be beneficial to her mentally and physically. So Mary Lincoln, restless, hoping to find forgetfulness in travel abroad, went to France, to Germany, to Italy. At Pau, France, in December, 1879, she fell from a stepladder while hanging a small picture over her mantelpiece and seriously injured her spine. Fearing now that she might die among strangers, in October, 1880, she sailed for America. Her nephew met her in New York and escorted her back to Springfield to the home of her sister, Mrs. Edwards. There, shrinking and sensitive, seeing no one—even when she was persuaded to take a drive the carriage curtains must be drawn—she spent the remainder of her broken, clouded life in the home filled with memories of her sparkling, happy girlhood, her rose-colored dreams of love and life. Prostrated by illness, the light of life and joy blotted out for her, she lingered in a purple twilight of grief until merciful death claimed her; the death she prayed for. "Ah, my dear friend," she wrote, "you will rejoice when you know that I have gone to my husband and children."

The end of her suffering came July 16, 1882. Her friends paid her silent tribute in the same room which had witnessed her light-hearted gayety and her marriage to the man of her choice, by whose side they reverently laid her. And could she have been conscious, with her slow, irradiating smile she would have said, "At last I am content—happy."

THE END

INDEX

NEW YORK

Publishers of BOOKS and of
HARPER'S MAGAZINE
—
Established 1817